HOW TO PREPARE FOR THE JOURNEY:
VOLUME II

Death, Dying, & Beyond

BY AL MINER AND LAMA SING

Death, Dying, and Beyond – How to Prepare for the Journey: Vol I

3rd Edition 2017

Cover art and book design by Susan M. Miner

ISBN-13 978-0-9791262-0-8

1. Lama Sing 2. Psychics 3. Trance Channel 4. Death and Dying
I. Miner, Al II. Title

Library of Congress Control Number: 2006909909

Printed in the United States of America

For books and products, further information, or to write Al Miner visit **www.lamasing.net**

On the edge of every person's consciousness
ever dwells one question:

What lies Beyond?

—Lama Sing

TABLE OF CONTENTS

Editor's Notes:

With the exception of a few words here and there, what you are about to read are the words of Lama Sing given in separate sessions (called readings), channeled by Al Miner. Questions that were sent in by the sponsor were read by Al at the opening, after which he placed himself into the trance state. Lama Sing would then enter the dimension of Earth, borrowing Al's voice for the reading.

Even though the name Lama Sing has been assigned to these readings, there is actually always a group involved. Depending upon the topic, sometimes the number is massive, and sometimes it is a handful; sometimes they are speaking to a group, and sometimes to an individual they know will one day get the message – in essence, speaking to one and all, as well as to only one and only all… curious, but true. Throughout the reading, they defer to one another just as we do when in a group discussion. This information may be of value as you read, so you don't stumble when they sometimes change, even in a single paragraph, from an archaic form of speech to a more modern one, or from the singular to the plural.

The name Channel is used by Lama Sing in place of Al, because to use the name Al would essentially serve to call him – call him from that consciousness to which he is taken that prevents his personal involvement and influence in what is given in the reading. There is only one known occasion in which Lama Sing used Al's given name. The reason given was that the depth of his channeled state was being tested.

Lastly…

There are places where Lama Sing emphasizes a thought by speaking the words quote/end-quote. To let the reader know that those emphases are Lama Sing's, as opposed to the transcriber's, the words quote/end-quote have been kept in the text as well as the quotation marks themselves.

The word dis-ease is used by Lama Sing to mean, not only illness and such, but "first and foremost, a lack of ease in spirit, mind, and/or emotion, which are then precipitated into the physical body."

Lama Sing's use of words such as ye, thee, whom, and he is often contrary to conventional, but the meaning will be clear.

As we commence with these works, we shall first pray in this manner:

Lord God, we ask of Thee in humbleness that Thou would guide us in this and all such works as we seek to endeavor on behalf of others. As you guide us, Father, now and throughout all of existence, help us to see the light of Thy spirit shining upon that path which is aright and purposeful in Thy name. We pray that you would grant us the presence of the Master, the Christ, so as to impart His healing grace, love, compassion and wisdom unto these works and all those who are gathered about same. And so do we, as well, offer this prayer on behalf of all those souls in all realms who are presently in some need and for whom there are none in joyful prayer. Humbly we thank Thee, Father, for this opportunity of joyful service in your name. Amen.

–Lama Sing

Reading One:

The Experiences of Death And Life Thereafter

This reading was given February 6, 1976 before an audience of approximately 150. The questions in this reading were submitted by members of the audience, with occasional follow-up questions of the audience by the conductor.

CONDUCTOR: You shall have before you, then, all things past, present, and future that shall have the greatest possible bearing on this group's development in this the physical plane, the spiritual plane, and the mental plane. You will go to a level best suited for a topical reading, asking for assistance from all those who can serve on those planes, asking for all that is able to be given on this topic as benefits directly those souls present.

This all shall be done in God's Name through the Master. The topic will be "the experience of death and life thereafter."

You will go then to this level of mindfulness from where you will obtain all information requested and answer any questions regarding same.

[Followed by countdown into deep trance state.]

LAMA SING COMMENTARY

Yes, we have the Channel, then, as well as those influences past, present, and future, as apply to that of your group gathered, and as well to the topic of *the departure of the physical body; and eternal life*, its experience, of course, never ending and without beginning. In the sense that God is eternal, so, then, are each of thee.

OPENING COMMENTS

In a sense, one who considers the departure from the physical body with fear or apprehension is, in essence, perhaps defining within themselves some discomfort with the lifetime experiences that have led to that point and not the event of departure from the flesh body itself.

To a large extent this is proper, for once the flesh body has been lain aside the *proper* body (or eternal body) is free to continue on determining its pathways and its purposes. But for an indefinable time, the body will encounter additional experiences that relate strongly to the lifetime just past. These are largely the product of that entity's experiences and attitudes in the mind and in the heart during that lifetime.

Living a Lifetime of Goodness

It becomes, then, quite obvious that the importance of living a lifetime of goodness for self and others takes on a duality of purpose. Certainly, the holy writings are clear in the need for this in the physical sense and imply clearly the aftereffects of such an attitude, but what has been removed from this Book is perhaps the most important point for you all:

The life after departure from the body is one that is experienced, built by the mind directly, without the time necessary in the Earth plane for the reality of thought to become solidified. Your thoughts become the framework of the reality that you exist in, and the collective thought and attitudes that have been manifested during your life just past become, in a sense, the world about you. It is that an errant thought will create a massive being that you must deal with but, rather, that the general scope of that attitude and of its emanations create the surroundings, in general, that you will encounter.

A Lifetime Completed

Death in the sense of that term in your plane implies a finality of being; in the truth of God's being, there is no death. There is oblivion that can only be chosen by the soul itself, one who would choose not to accept their eternal nature. This, too, can only last for a time, after which the soul is awakened and finds itself gathered in a position wherein those of loving nature (guides and such) attempt to bring it into the realization that it continues its existence.

So many of you who have had loved ones on the Earth plane depart from your side have pondered why this one or that one should leave at a particular time. It is not what you would call accidental or random selection. It is, rather, that these souls in the majority of cases have completed their task for that lifetime and, therefore, have no further need of that body nor its confining nature.

Yes, there are sorrows that are felt by that departed one but not for the loss of that physical body. It would be sorrow that there cannot be the continuation of assistance to others.

Importance of Prayer

The use of prayer is so very important here, dear friends, for prayer is a form of thought and energy that is not restricted to any particular level, realm, or sphere. It can transcend the densest matter and rise to the most rare or purified levels. Very little else, save those of high levels of acceptance of God, can accomplish this. Prayer is a form of God's Grace in action.

It is the Living God, permitted through thy works and these to be manifested on behalf of thee and others.

Reincarnation

There are so many areas of discussion within this particular topic that we have pondered for some time which ones to select. Since there is so much interest in your present time in the Earth plane in the topic of reincarnative experiences, and this does relate closely to the life/death pattern of physical body, this cannot go unmentioned:

At the conclusion of your life experiences and upon the completion of what you would call certain entry requirements to other planes, you will proceed to assess your past experiences in that just previous lifetime, merging them and comparing them to the totality of your experiences from (what we shall call) the soul's memory. This, then, is assessed and you judge yourself, in a manner of speaking. You may do this in complete seclusion, though ever present are those who are available to counsel thee and to listen to your comments and point out any errors in your judgment.

Upon the culmination of this, it will become your right to choose to enter again a form of existence that will enable you to experience and grow, for it is written that the grandest of tools for building serves no merit unless they are used.

Therefore, the experiences on Earth offer one of the greatest honors to each of you, as you have the opportunity to use that which is given.

Karma

Karmic ties have their influence here, though we hasten to add that karma is neither bad nor good. It simply exists. It is the force of being that continues to urge and prod you towards balancing with events past and those planned for future which has the insistence of being met. It can be placed aside for a period of time, but it must be understood within thy being.

It does not mean that for a karmic action in a past lifetime one must live an entire lifetime in repayment, for time is not of the significance that you purport it to be on your plane. It is, rather, that you progress in one, two, or twenty lifetimes, until your mind and heart are merged in the understanding of the completeness of that karmic action.

Once this is accomplished--and it may be so in one day's existence or one-hundred-thousand days; your choice, you see--then the karmic pattern is balanced, and you will choose to go on from the position that you will accept.

We believe that this, in humbleness then, should be our point of conclusion, so as to accept any questions forthcoming from your gathering.

QUESTIONS & ANSWERS

QUESTION 1: *What cannot be done on the next plane that we can do here, now, and should be concerned about?*

LAMA SING: You will find it very difficult to define any particular thing that cannot be done in what you call the next world because, again, dependent upon your cumulative attitude and thought, you have built that world. You see? Such in the example of, let us say, an entity on the Earth plane in physical body who has become deeply involved with some desire for foodstuffs or what you call fermented beverages may find themselves still desiring same after the departure of their physical body.

This would cause them to dwell often very close to the Earth realm, for the reality of this cannot be found in these realms beyond the physical; the mental sense of this can, but the entity dwells in, in a sense, what is called a living hell, for they have all that they wish but it does not gratify.

It is like the man we saw who had all the money he wanted but no one was interested in it in his realm. So after the passage of some several hundred years, he realized that he had no further desire for this. He was ready, then, to move forward in his progression, and loving souls were present to guide.

Q 1-2: *In other words, you are saying that we have to balance with that kind of thing in this lifetime?*

LAMA SING: You should balance with those elements of yourself that are out of balance. That is to say, if any particular trait within you is not in moderation, then this may be a deterrent preventing full spiritual awareness. So, try to search yourself for balance. Do not attach, too strongly, importance to the physical aspects of the Earth plane.

Q 1-3: *What if we were not capable of balancing within this lifetime? Or, let us say, we met an untimely death where we had not balanced within? How could we approach it then from that plane? How would we handle it there?*

LAMA SING: Always remember that God is, ever, loving and that He would not abandon thee. If it were not by thy choice that thy departure from the Earth plane occurred, then, you would receive immediate opportunity to return to the Earth plane before any undue anguish or any form of suffering could take place. You would simply, in the soul's sense of this, be in harmony or slumber until the opportunity for an additional life would be presented.

Q 1-2: *What of habits, such as smoking?*

LAMASING: This is one habit that we might include in this (with a note of humor), for you would find that you would have ample abundance of these, if it were strong enough in your mind, but they would not gratify as they did in the Earth plane. For this is related to the Earth plane; it is not related to those planes beyond. Though the image and the full expression of this might be found, it would not provide thee the same gratification. After a time, it would become very boring for you and you would forget about it and move on.

QUESTION 2: *How is pain registered on the other side? Is it simply anguish there or is there something akin to bodily hurt, as we know it?*

LAMA SING: There is a semblance of certain fears of bodily pain, though you must understand that this is, in a sense, imagined. It is that the mind has built the world or determined the world that they shall live in. In this, there may be hostilities and bodily harm may be a part of this. There would be the same effect as the suffering, but there would not be the loss to the body, for the body is eternal at that point. (Unless, of course, there was a reincarnation experience wherein a body was resumed.)

No pain to those who defy pain, no hell for those who will not accept this portion of the mind's work.

QUESTION 3: *Do some entities leave the Earth plane because they were on the wrong pathway or entered at the wrong time? Please give an example.*

LAMA SING: On occasion, yes, this has occurred, though it is extremely rare. Based on the full review of one's past experiences, that one may determine that to enter the Earth plane at a particular point in Earth time is very beneficial and, therein, selects a situation and a moment close to time of birth only to find that the situations about these entities have abruptly changed. You would, then, have the opportunity to depart before what would be customary.

This is very often found in what you call crib deaths, where the departure of the soul is very abrupt. In other instances, there are souls who enter the Earth plane with the full knowledge that this will be a short time span on the Earth plane. For example, one might choose a short span for the benefit of another, or of a group, or a mass populous, or the general mind of man such as those who enter the Earth plane knowing they shall be involved in one of your classics of mind called war.

QUESTION 4: *If entities can and do choose to enter the Earth plane, is there any relationship to what is considered a truly accidental death of that entity, such as through a freak accident?*

LAMA SING: There are those cases, under certain circumstances, wherein an entity can lose the vehicle (or body) they were occupying through no intent of their own. But this is not the normal. It is abnormal. These entities, then, are given what you would call first priority to reenter the Earth plane, if it is their choice.

Q 4-2: *How quickly sometimes do they reincarnate?*

LAMASING: Of all those references that you have lovingly requested from this gathering in a case of an involuntary departure, the earliest that we have found to this time has been several hours. But this is extremely unusual. It is, rather, that the conditions were proper for that soul and hence the opportunity was provided.

QUESTION 5: *How does suicide fit in?*

LAMA SING: The term suicide amuses us here. And please try to understand this, dear friends. It is that the entity will attempt to depart from the difficulties of the Earth plane and look for some eternal sleep or oblivion. When they do awaken, my! It is such a start! They have not comprehended what has transpired, and it takes a considerable effort to help them understand that they are not dead. Nor are they in the place of the gentleman with the red garment. Nor are they in any such place where they will not find opportunity to return and deliberate the issue of this route previously pursued.

Q 5-2: *They will have to return again to go back to the same problem that they had before they committed suicide, correct?*

LAMA SING: This is very much so, but it is their own choice to so do. It regards what you would call their *chosen pathway* when they had chosen to depart. They will, then, wish to return.

Q 5-3: *Would they choose that situation in their next reincarnation?*

LAMA SING: Not always. Here again, these entities are usually given first priority, though we do not wish to give the impression that this term implies; they are *usually* fairly rapid in returning, though some who have particularly strong mental anguish may live in their darkness for a period of several hundreds of years, your time measurement. Then, when the circumstances are capable of being dealt with, would return.

QUESTION 6: *Once a person has become old and senile and has to be taken care of as though an infant, what purpose does the soul have in forcing a useless body to continue its existence? What can the soul learn if the mind and body are useless?*

LAMA SING: This soul is performing what is called, at that point, a benevolent act.

Bear in mind, dear friends, that it is not always a joy to remain on the Earth plane. These souls are acting on the need of, and loving kindness to, other souls yet remaining in the Earth plane. Consider that those who are learning through this experience could not obtain this knowledge in any other singular way.

Also, the presence of their soul or spiritual force on the Earth plane, even though their mind and body may not seem alert by your standards, may be involved in great works with others who are in duress on the Earth plane. Very, very often many of the spiritual forces that are felt in the Earth plane in healing works are these same entities who benevolently retain their bodies just to be present with their spiritual force to give light, as with the Master to those brethren in need. Think again next when you are in the presence of one such!

Q 6-2: *Don't, many times, these people remain on Earth because they are tied by the love of someone for them, such as family?*

LAMA SING: Your statement is quite correct. We have recently encountered one such entity who was literally bound to their body by the love, or mourning, of his loved ones.

You must realize that the journeys on the Earth plane are very brief, and when they are completed, the entity should be wished a good journe, sent with love and with prayer, of course.

QUESTION 7: *You say that when people die, in a majority of cases, it is because they have achieved what they came here to achieve and, therefore, move on. What other reasons would there be for dying?*

LAMA SING: In such cases as individuals are not learning well their chosen pathways and have allowed the physical forms to reduce themselves beyond the useable point, that the pathway that was chosen cannot be completed within the vehicle that is present at that time, this may cause a departure; the ineffectual use of the tools that one has at hand; the avoidance of gifts that are given to that soul for purpose of benefit to others; unusual acts which do not honor Universal Laws; and, occasionally, accidental influence to depart the Earth plane… These are perhaps among the major causes of what you would call death.

QUESTION 8: L*ama Sing, please explain the importance of attitude in life and how attitude may affect the progression of a soul soon after physical death.*

LAMA SING: This cannot be stressed heavily enough, dear friends. After the death of a body, it is the will of your existence that you have built with your own attitude that you will see first. If you have been a kind and thoughtful person, to *yourself* as well as others, you will find this to be the environ that you will experience.

This is one reason why this group humbly often states that you must love yourselves, for *thou* art the living God as well as thy neighbors. If you do not love yourself in your lifetime, this adversity within self will be experienced immediately after death. You will face it, dear friends. This has priority, perhaps over any other item of experience or attitude in the general sense.

Following this, you will build your own image, in a sense, that which you will accept of yourself. Then, you will move from this place into the experiencing of the attitudes that you have maintained through that lifetime. You will spend an indefinable period of time in that existence built by your attitude. Thereafter, once you have accomplished your understanding of them, you will move into realms where you can evaluate these against your total being's experience.

QUESTION 9: *Do we have the authority to release another from karma created in an action toward or against us? Is this a benefit to us only or to the offender also?*

LAMA SING: You seem to know the answer here but we thank thee for presenting the question. It is certainly one worthwhile, indeed: the release of karmic ties.

Let us say that one on the Earth plane has offended thee grievously. Since your attitude toward that entity must be present in order to form a karmic link of any stature, you certainly do have the opportunity to release that entity, to a large degree, from a karmic tie. It will remain up to them to accept this or not

But they cannot involve you in that karmic tie if you forgive them. If your heart and mind are pure enough, more likely than not, your influence and effect will have sufficient benefit upon them that you will help them to see the wisdom of releasing that karma. If you are successful in that, you will reap a very fine harvest, for this is extremely illuminating to your soul's position with God.

We cannot overemphasize the purpose and lessons obtained in forgiveness, dear friends. One who can forgive will truly walk at the Master's side. None would stand higher than this one.

QUESTION 10: *Is there to be a Resurrection Day, when Christ will come and gather all those together? Is the body raised into a spiritual body and gathered together by Christ into a place called Heaven. Does your soul go to be with God upon death, and is this called Resurrection Day?*

LAMA SING: Your soul never leaves its position with God. Your soul is always in accord with God. (This is given to you to define the purpose of spiritual searching.)

The Resurrection is that purpose for seeking the Christ Light within [note, below]. It is this Light, and this alone, that can bring to the mind and heart of an aware entity in physical body the full realization of the nature of their being.

The Resurrection, then, was rightly called in these terms, as it was originally stated in great lengths how to achieve complete union with the force of God and the love and kindness of the Master as manifested by God.

In this, then, you will have a Resurrection. It is planned. It is the purpose of your continued evolution. But in the sense that your physical body would be "raised," the physical body is merely the collection of matter which has been formed by thought and has drawn upon the forces of the plane that you exist in, and given unto the materials of thought formation, and composited into a form that agrees with the rules or accepted thought of that plane.

It would not be logical for you to wish to reassemble that physical body, when the true body that is yours has far more beauty and cannot be harmed or injured when your mind is elevated to its position with God.

[Note: Christ/the Master – The Christ Spirit is that infinite eternal essence that is the continuity of God's intent borne in each of His Children. The Christ is a Principle. It is a spirit. It is the life. The Master has brought this Christ Consciousness into oneness with Himself. Thus, He has become the Christ. Just so many stumble over this. –Lama Sing]

QUESTION 11: *When a person is in a coma for a very long time and is apparently wasting away, kept alive through machines, is that against the natural law? Is the soul's time up, and should it be released?*

LAMA SING: The question truly asks, can one truly force a Child of God to remain if they do not wish? We believe the answer to this is obvious.

You can sustain the physical body, but we assure you, you cannot captivate a soul--all souls, all beings, belong to God--no more than you could encaptivate God within a sheath.

QUESTION 12: *What determines true death on this plane? Is it the loss of heartbeat, loss of brain waves? And again, what of individuals who are kept alive through the functioning of a machine?*

LAMA SING: We assume that you are referring to those who are simply in existence in the physical sense. The definitive measurement would be the presence of the spirit of that entity in that body. If the spirit is not present, you merely have a combination of chemicals functioning in a pre-ordained method on the Earth plane, you see?

Q 12-2: *Is there any way that you can tell us how we can tell if the spirit was still present, or not?*

LAMA SING: If the spirit is present, it will respond to prayer. It will respond to love. It will respond in a definable energy pattern. This energy pattern can be seen by certain entities who are unrestricted in their vision in that way, and it is possible to detect this by instrumentation.

Q 12-3: *Someone who would be able to see it... what could they see? And what kind of a machine can detect that, Lama Sing?*

LAMA SING: They would see the auric field, the presence of the spirit about that entity. We are not speaking of the life force, which is very close to the body itself but the auric field, which is the activity of that spirit working in that body.

A device, which would employ (among other possible types of mechanisms) would use something similar to an argon tube, using crystal rectifiers and the like for amplification and control; also using baffle type deflectors.

Also this can be detected through the use of certain forms of electro-engraving photography as is quite commonplace (and we ponder that this has not been employed as yet). It is referred to commonly as Kirlian photography.

QUESTION 13: *What is the best attitude one could have when facing the death transition?*

LAMA SING: Well (with a small note of humor), this largely depends upon the attitude that has been maintained previously, you see. That is to say that, if one has lived a lifetime that they will be pleased to review, they should look upon the experience of death of the physical body as one very joyous. And it is true, dear friends, that even though there may have been errant ways in that lifetime, this, too, should be placed aside. One must learn to forgive self and to accept God's blessings and His forgiveness. Thusly, we could reiterate, in these humble ways:

Consider the very many times that you have realized for a brief moment that you are eternal, that you have realized that some bond exists between thee and all other entities that you have not been capable of defining. Remember that, as the mind is the builder, there must be some power to the mind that is eternal in nature, that this is the expressive portion of the spirit that the spirit then will sum itself up.

Before the pressures and effects of the physical departure can truly have an effect upon you, you will have departed. It is a joyful experience. It is one that should be looked at with a joyous reverence. It is much similar to returning to a place that has been very dear to you in past. It is like going home.

QUESTION 14: *How is it explained as the soul's desire to leave the Earth plane when the conscious mind and physical body seems to want to live here so desperately, such as cancer or leukemia victims?*

LAMA SING: Yes, this particular area of dis-ease is a matter that greatly concerns souls involved with the Earth plane. This dis-ease, as it is called, is a large contribution of the mass-mind thought.

There is no such dis-ease other than that that exists in the minds of man! It is through thy own willingness, dear friends, that such manifestations occur.

It is, of course, detectable in the sense that an activity has taken place but, then, a thought is detectable, is it not? Thoughts, permeating throughout the body and surrounding physical forms in your cities and in your places of sadness and the like do take their toll, you see, and they are not indiscriminate. They will select an opening (such as a moment of sadness allows, a doubt, or a thought) to enter. This can have its effect.

Q 14-2: *Do you have any further comment on that, Lama Sing?*

LAMA SING: This particular dis-ease is perhaps singularly the easiest one for those of you who understand your own abilities and position with God as what you call healers in terms of that which you can conquer, for it exists in mind alone.

The reaction with the cerebral-spinal system and its related systems and its interaction with the ductless glands do have the secretive ability of toxins, which cannot be destroyed externally, for they are internally produced. (My, my. It is taking your white-coated gentlemen a long time to figure that one out, is it not?)

QUESTION 15: *Did the earthquake in Guatemala have any relationship to the inhabitants of that area, or was that loss of life strictly a consequence of Earth changes?*

LAMA SING: Loss of life in that expression of the

Earth plane was as was predicted. This was a part of the Earth Changes. And these will be increasing (changes) from this point forward, as we discussed sometime previously. We do not wish to give the impression that this was a condemnation of certain groups of souls. Many of these knew well in advance of this forthcoming event. It was their choice, you see.

Q 15-2: They knew? Conscious mind or subconscious mind?

LAMA SING: Both. Many knew consciously of this forthcoming event.

QUESTION 16: *From what part of the body is the death hormone secreted? How long, in our time, does it take to complete its function?*

LAMA SING: This question relates to the previous question as to the righteousness of maintaining a physical body. You cannot counteract that which is called in this question the *death hormone*, for it is the absence of the life hormone, in a sense, combined with toxins, which are released to completely free the life force from the body.

It can be some several hours time before the last of the life force is gone, in the Earth plane sense of this. For some, cells can "live" (in that sense of the term) for even longer periods. But the spiritual portion of thy being, or the true body, takes but several moments to depart... once it has determined it, you see. And it is clearly visible to the eyes of those who accept God. It is measurable to the extent of certain electron changes and in variation of weight, temperature, and an internal shock to the cerebral-spinal, as is the release of the spirit to the life form or physical body.

QUESTION 17: *After death, how many levels does a soul travel before reincarnation?*

LAMA SING: This is dependent upon that soul's acceptance of God and its ability to utilize those tools and materials that would prove to itself its ability to function on different levels. There are infinite levels in that sense. For there are infinite series of thoughts, and there must be, then, that place for that position wherein each group of thoughts can function.

But in the general sense, a soul will commune with its own spirit. That is to say, wherever that soul's position is in its own acceptance of God, that is the level which would be attained. (This can vary very much, indeed.)

QUESTION 18: *Please tell us why, in areas where the earthquake such as just happened, all the souls that made their transition occurred at one time. Is this God's Plan? What happens to all of them?*

LAMA SING: In a sense, it is God's Plan, but we would not state it in the definitive sense of one plotting and calculating certain events. It is that God's infinite wisdom would know all these things.

Largely, this group of souls departed at this time as was chosen and will enter a period of re-awareness or re-awakening and will return to the Earth plane relatively soon, in ten to fifteen years time. These souls, then, will be considered as a part of the greater groups serving in the Master's Light during that time which is before thee. (Largely of Atlantean origin, to answer the question that is in the minds of several in your group.)

QUESTION 19: *What are your thoughts on modern day funerals, Lama Sing? Describe a better way and attitude that should be practiced at this time.*

LAMA SING: We wish to retain an attitude of respect with you, dear friends, but you must understand that much of this is paganistic in its nature. It is, rather, that one might very well celebrate the achievement of another soul who has gone forward, rather than mourn them so grievously… and to give honor to them, of course.

But the sadness should be as it was by many of your

peoples, your native Americans, some eight to fifteen hundred years previously. In this, you might find some illumination. These native American Indians often would place themselves around the body of a departed comrade and would be made to sit before this body for day after day until they could completely release all thoughts that they held for this entity, both good or bad. Until they could, with a clear heart, send love and wish that entity well in his next life, the entity was not permitted to be consumed. The entities holding this bond were identified by those who were aware of such things. It could often be many, many days before the entity was allowed to be consumed by the forces from which he was created.

The moral of the story is this: that to tie one's mental thoughts to another entity, in the aspect that one would hold them to the Earth plane, is a very difficult thing to unravel for them when they arrive in other realms. It is diminishing to their strength. It is clouding to their awareness. They would pray for thee diligently not only to release them but to find the complete joy and happiness that is yours. So, perhaps a ceremony might consist of some of those points.

We understand the love that is involved here. We would only suggest that, when you depart from the ceremony, please leave any bonds, any ties, there. Think only wishes of continued journey and good happiness awaiting the time when you can commune with them again.

QUESTION 20: *What is your attitude on cremation?*

LAMA SING: Well, we can't see that it matters whether it be chemicals or arranged in a box or in a bottle.

The theory that many have in regard to this is that they will lose their position at an appointed time. Would thou thinkest God would forget thee quite that easily? And did He not state that it was from dust that originally you came? Certainly understand that He has maintained the plans for you and can rebuild you if necessary.

QUESTION 21: *Please describe the next plane. Does it have time and space? Does it exist on other planets? Approximately how many different planes are there?*

LAMA SING: The existence of future planes, as we have come to call them, is dependent upon the attitudes and emotive extent of the entities' activities, collectively, in the past. In a general sense, an entity will experience time and space and will have found they entered into an existence much in the same form as you have at present. However, you will find that the body is much more hearty, capable of sustaining itself.

The experiences on different planes vary so greatly that this would require a topic in itself to cover. Some planes have existence in the form of what you would call light, sound, and vibration. Other planes have existence in exactly the same bodily form as you have at present. Yet others may exist in whatsoever form they choose, for their evolution is such that they are experimenting with awareness and would form themselves in harmony with whatever they find at hand. This, of course, was the original position of many souls when they first became encaptivated in flesh bodies on the Earth plane, as many of you know.

The journeying to other planets and spheres involved with same is a very distinct reality. Many, many other planets have life forms very identical to yours. Many of them are lesser in their progression, and a good number of them are very far advanced in terms of their awareness. \\\Your own planet was the home for many of these in a timeframe beyond your comprehension. In this, then, you would find much that your heritage is seemingly urging you towards stems from their influence and their prayers or mental thoughts towards you and all others in your universe.

… Yes, we have your question, my friend, speaking to a thought from one in the audience: In regards to this, yes you can reincarnate to that planet if you are acceptable to that existence, if your mind and your emotive attitudes are such that you are acceptable, yes. It is similar to vibrating frequencies. If your vibrations, in essence, can exist in that sphere, you can exist there and you can choose to have an experience there, you see?

[pause]

...Very well, yes... It was the planet you are referring to... To our writer friend.

QUESTION 22: *Lama Sing, from a previous statement, explain: "the body being consumed after death by what the body is created of." What does that mean?*

LAMA SING: Those forces which exist in your plane of reference, the Earth plane, consist of certain vibratory lengths and energy patterns. It is a natural law that these vibrations tend to return to their original form. Is it not? We believe this is one of your laws of physics: All things tend to emanate back to their original form.

In this, your body is little different. All the various elements that are the composite of your body would tend to return to itself. Thus, the body would be consumed by its own origin, you see?

Q 22-2: *If we do not learn our lessons, so to speak, do we continually return to the Earth over and over again?*

LAMA SING: Not necessarily. You may choose to engage in those activities that will provide for greater learning on non-physical planes or other physical planes. There are quite a number of these.

QUESTION 23: *Is it true that souls or some souls stay on another plane called Arcturus before choosing another plane of expression? And can a soul use another plane to improve itself enough never to return to the Earth plane or another plane?*

LAMA SING: You are referring to what we would call the intermediary stop in a single plane. This Arcturus, then, is a position from whence entities usually move to spheres of reference well beyond the vibrational capability of the Earth plane.

From this point it is very rare that entities will return to the Earth plane. Though it is permitted, it is not likely that this will occur. It is not required that they would return to any physical reincarnation, though certainly they will continue on in experiencing in different planes of awareness.

(…We are approaching the time when it will become necessary to release the Channel. Please be advised.)

Q 23-2: T*hen isn't it only a matter of desire? Ideal is here, to get rid of all bad desires, then, this accomplished, rid one's self of all desire?*

LAMA SING: Not completely, in the structure of those verbiages. The balance is what we are striving for, you see. One cannot have life without such. We are not looking for what you would call extremes, however. We are trying to point out to you that it is imperative that you balance your desires. Without desires, without purpose and ideals and goals, what have we, dear friends? Mannequins. We would not choose this, and, certainly, God has not chosen to have us be partners with Him as mannequins. Therefore, it is important that you balance with those influences, striving always for harmony between urgings and desires and those feelings of necessity.

Balance yourselves in all aspects. Eliminate from your mind (as best as you can, of course) lust and greed and try to replace them with understanding and love. For love is truly the Master's Way in existence, and love and understanding is in essence the fiber of God's Being. It is very important that you understand that it is not the total elimination of any thing but, rather, the balance.

QUESTION 24: *Is it wrong to be buried or cremated before being dead three days?*

LAMA SING: It is unwise in many cases, as the entity may not be fully dead in the sense of many religions and prophecies. There are those entities who can suspend themselves for even beyond this.

In the sense of the definition and relationship to the writings of the Master, we would not consider that any action itself be wrong or sinful, save that which is a breach or blockage between self and God for this prevents the entity from accepting and living in their rightful heritage, you see?

Q 24-2: *What about embalming, Lama Sing?*

LAMA SING: One moment please.

[pause].

Yes, very well. In regard to this we are advised that we have limited reference to this particular action. What we are given is that it would be, from this group's reference at present, more advisable for anointing than embalming. In view of the activities in the Earth plane in certain peoples, we consider this more viable.

QUESTION 25: *If forgiveness is the highest trait that an entity can attain, does this mean that punishment—including the death penalty—is not for others to inflict on persons in this plane?*

LAMA SING: One must understand that the Master functioned in the realm wherein He existed. Thou must do the like, wherever you exist. Do you exist in a realm wherein understanding and love are the rules? If so, abide by them. Keep within self, always, those tenets which thou knowest to be true and right. But where thou dwellest, abide by the laws of man as best you can where they do not interfere or violate those Laws of God.

Thou shalt not kill is something to consider here. We would not suggest the willful death of another. But in man's laws we see this necessity, and be appraised that many souls are aware of this when they enter the Earth plane. That may, in effect, be just what they need at that point in time. (Though this group does not recommend that action, humbly speaking.)

QUESTION 26: *I would ask if you have any closing statements and, after that, since you point out again the need for prayer, the most powerful thing we have, would you at the close give us one of your beautiful prayers, and perhaps the chant you use that everyone so enjoys.*

LAMA SING: We will request permission to do these things.

[pause]

CLOSING COMMENTS

In closing, then, we would state to you, dear friends, that it is our prayer we have helped you to understand the natural evolution of your spirit, for your life in a physical body is the movement of your spirit through time. It is: as the wind caresses the leaves of your land, so does your spirit caress innumerable bodies, in innumerable lands. Your spirit is as free as that wind and as wondrous and warming to behold. Never lose sight of the spiritual aspect of your being.

Understand that each entity near thee at this time is dealing with certain points of balance at their soul's reference point. Be, ever, loving in your understanding towards them, and know them. Be kindly to them, that they will progress, and note how they will take you with them just a step further.

We are permitted then, of course, to give this prayer at this time. (As to the request of the chant, as stated, this must be referred to at another time. In such, then, we would advise that no other contacts [readings] would be made for that twenty-four hour period preceding.)

Closing Prayer

We ask now, O Father, that each of these children of Thy flock be awakened within their being. We beseech Thee, that they may see within the temple where Thou livest within that they may know of the eternal nature of their being; that they will turn in their neighbor's hour of need and touch their hand, giving them Thy loving kindness; that they may comprehend the healing powers of Thy presence and that they will not fear nor restrict these from others; and that they will, in their darkest times, look upward within and see Thy Light as a comfort and joy reaching into all corners of their being, ever attempting to illuminate. We ask Thy love, Thy eternal blessings be known in their minds. All these things we ask in the Master's Name, knowing that so doing, so shall Thee manifest them.

And so, beloved friends, until we next meet – in thy slumber time, in thy waking hours, or in an action or deed in service to the Master – we bid thee fare well.

Reading Two:

How to Prepare for Departure from the Body
And Return to the True Body

This reading was given February 6, 1976.

—

LAMA SING COMMENTARY

What The Body Is

To prepare for the departure from the body is to recognize just what the body is.

Physical and Spiritual Expression

The physical form is a vehicle, as has been given here and by other servants in God's work. That which is inhabited within and about the body often referred to as the spirit and/or the soul is a continuous form or expression of life which began at the moment of God's conception of thee and which shall never conclude.

This then, might, in its general sense, be considered "the body," of sorts, and the emphasis placed upon the present life's pattern just as an experience, or as the vehicle with which one traverses from a given point in time/space to yet another point called the destination of that lifetime. Thus the *body* is the eternal nature of man: man's consciousness, man's awareness.

But even this, because it is described in words, is too limiting to describe thy true body. So very often entities will ask, genuinely thirsting for knowledge, "What form is my body? How shall I express myself after I have departed my present physical form?" The answer is a very difficult one to give, for it relates to the intentions and purposes that your soul has as its objectives after said departure. To state that you would have a physical form just as you have at present may limit thee. But it is true that your form is expressed for long periods of time (as you would measure it) in a form very similar to your physical form of present. So the body is, in essence, best described perhaps, humbly, as a form of consciousness not limited to the parameters or dimensions, breadth and depth, of your present physical structure.

With this thought in mind, recognizing that your true body is in essence as unlimited as the source of its creation, we would then continue.

The Cycle of Physical and Spiritual Bodies

It has been stated moments ago in conversation near where the Channel's body dwells that preparation for departure of the body actually begins at the moment of entry into that body … in short, at the moment of birth into the Earth plane.

We have, as well, given in past that, in a sense, birth into the Earth plane is a form of death in another realm. Ponder that just a moment. We have also stated that death in the Earth plane, though it be sad, may well be considered a worthy time of rejoicing as is the custom with certain religions and cultures in the Earth, for it is subsequently the rebirth into another realm.

So, here we find a pattern of death/birth, death/birth and again repeating itself as a cycle often defined in certain writings as "the cyclic nature of man in his spirit." Then the question, or true topic, before us at present might be: first, to recognize that this body exists; secondly, to determine what use it shall be put to during its duration of tenure in the Earth plane; and thirdly, the summation, preparation, transition and re-entry into other realms.

The Purpose of the Finite Expression

Having described somewhat the first, and having entered into the topic of the second, we should consider that use of the body physical is somewhat different than the use of the spiritual body.

The spiritual body has no confines in the sense of its nature, of its effectiveness, of its consciousness, of its awareness, its knowledge, wisdom, creative ability and so on. Conversely, the physical body is limited: in its ability to communicate, to express, to experience through travel, through encounters, in terms of its senses, in terms of its knowledge to that which has been gleaned and taught consciously, and so forth.

Then the question (and, perhaps, purpose for your life) might well be: Why is there a difference? Why does this beautiful body, which exists by God's Word, express in a finite or limited form? And why can we not join these two forms into one beautiful being?

Well, dear friends, once you arrive at that point (that question, asked within yourself), you are beginning to prepare yourself to truly receive God.

Preparing for Acceptance of God

Preparing for the departure from the body might well be called preparing for acceptance of God, in the sense that, as one recognizes (a step beyond the veil of darkness, or death), they still exist. At that moment there are resplendent reactions in some, aspects of horror and fright in others, feelings of unworthiness, frustration and failure in yet others, and a continuum of infinite experiences and combinations thereof, limited only to the conceptual imagination of mankind. In short, as many variations as you can muster.

Why all of this? Why do certain entities fear the action of transition? Then perhaps preparing for departure from the body might again, additionally, be thought of as preparing to cement a block into the foundation of thine own soul. Once you have departed an experience, the experience is completed: those experiences which you molded, fashioned, shaped. They can be adorned. They can be fired. They can be tempered in many ways. The choice is in the thought and attitude of the potter.

So, your life in the Earth plane, then, has the consistency of your own will. It has the flexibility, the malleability of your thought. The preparation is, in other words, a work, a labor, which is conceived at the spiritual/mental level and is enacted in the physical or Earth plane.

Preparing for Departure

Moving on then to the third aspect of the topic, the departure is a moment of truth for some. At that instant or moment, they realize that they will shortly discover whether or not there is truth to the fable of an existing God and life beyond the veil of darkness. (We chose to use the term "fable" for several reasons. The term denotes that of a tale carried on from generation to generation. It also denotes that which has some latitude in terms of repetition. And it also emphasizes the imaginative or creative qualities of both the teller and those who listen.)

In essence, again, that is the true body: that which is built by the thoughts and attitudes, our imaginations; and then the enactment of thought, generated through imagination into conscious thought, into directed purpose and, ultimately, daily life. This, then, becomes the fable, the story, and the belief. So awesome a moment to some as they review their entire lifetime, often related in terms of Earth plane time in such a way: In an instant my entire life unfolded before me. Unbelievable as it may sound, I truly reviewed my entire lifetime.

Each of you, no doubt, has either heard this expression, or perhaps, at a moment in time, experienced it to a greater or lesser extent. But time is measurable in seconds, minutes, hours, days, months, years. How is it possible to jam a lifetime into a few moments, or minutes, or even hours? Is it akin to a round hole in a square peg? They do not match. Thus there must be some difference, then. This is the difference between realms, dimensional, ordered realms, such as a three dimensional Earth plane, which exists as such because of its accord in terms of its inhabitants.

Beyond the Veil of Darkness

Just beyond the veil of darkness, then, is the moment's reflection, but this time, in that instant, it's not a review of the past lifetime, but a review of every experience that your soul has had from the moment of its conception to the present.

Then, how does one prepare to meet this moment? If all of this is, in fact, your destiny, and you are aware of this at this time, what should you, what can you, do to prepare for this? So very many teachings have been built around this. In fact, cultures, religions, societies, have been directed towards this very thought. Yet your world continues, as it must. Societies, governments, are fashioned from various fragments, and life seems to obscure this very beautiful, awesome, moment of your life … one which you know you shall meet inevitably, yet it is so distant and so unreal.

Meeting this moment can be now. Meeting this decision, this choice, this review, can be, in a minute way, a part of your daily life. It would not be in a fearsome, remorseful, despondent way but, rather, in a sense of joyous anticipation wherein you would strive to make this lifetime be a building-stone in the structure of your own being which is beautifully hewn and polished: so that every experience glimmers and shimmers, as the facet of a beautiful gem; so that it has a strength, a cohesion quality which is unexcelled; and so that it is the very finest of experiences which you can contribute to your soul structure, and thus recognizing that each is a part of the other. This structure and this building-block (or this symbol of building) contributes in the same beautiful way towards the whole.

So very much, indeed, we would wish to share with you and to give to you to guide you, but we must honor these questions which have been brought before this humble group, and ask prayerfully that these bring forward the questions in the hearts and minds of each of you who shall follow. With this thought then, we would welcome your questions.

QUESTIONS & ANSWERS

QUESTION 1: *What thoughts should we hold at the time of death?*

LAMA SING: It is so very important to hold the correct thoughts throughout life, so that the action or experience of death has very little effect upon the emotions, upon the mind, and that there can be a loving attitude given to others around you at this time, as much or moreso than any other.

Hold the thought which is thy highest ideal.

Throughout your life, frequently meditate and pray, and reflect upon the ideal which you believe in. You know God to exist because you have practiced believing during your lifetime and, in this belief, you have been given within yourself and, in many ways, what you need in terms of evidence to support this belief and to encourage the continuation of it.

A period of meditation, yes; a period of awareness, yes; a period of perpetuation of the highest which has been practiced during that lifetime: Hold this, then, in thought.

QUESTION 2: *Does preparing for departure vary with different individuals? And if so, how can we best determine how to prepare as an individual?*

LAMA SING: This varies to the extent that each is individual. That is, the ideal which would be held, the images, the mental and spiritual awareness, would vary somewhat for each. And that is why, in so many teachings that you will find in the Earth plane, you are encouraged to look within … so that you would find your ultimate support and guidance from the presence of God within yourself.

You can uphold and support another entity's belief. You can contribute in forms of labor, in forms of love, in every way, to a common goal and bond. But, ultimately, you shall bring a very beautiful and unique ingredient to the sum of that group purpose, and that is your own individual nature as a unique soul created by God, which, in the same manner as given moments ago, reflect within!

Find the purposes, goals, not only in the material or physical sense, but in the spiritual, eternal sense. Reflect upon what works, what functions, would be those which you would find to be in harmony with you eternally.

QUESTION 3: *What of those who are taken abruptly as through accidents, when in just the blink of an eye they are gone over, and they don't even know that they are going over? How do they prepare? Are they able to prepare themselves in that brief period of time? Or just by way of life they are always preparing?*

LAMA SING: In the instant of what we would consider to be a true accident, that is expanded just in the manner which we gave initially, where, in a moment, one's lifetime proceeds by his consciousness, as though viewed in a theatre or cinema, and he has, in many cases, various choices. But in the case of a true accident, these souls are given very, very quick opportunities to return to the Earth plane, to resume the purposes of that lifetime if they were incomplete.

Now, in the majority of what you would term accident, these entities know well in advance of the impending activity which is to terminate their physical body's existence, and have, at other various levels of consciousness, fully prepared for this event. This can be seen in those entities who, in a moment, will volunteer their own life to save another, those who would risk all that they have to assure that another will continue to live.

The preparation is not just a momentary action. It, rather, should be a life's endeavor.

QUESTION 4: *Would you please outline the best procedure to follow, in order to assist others at the time of their transition? In other words, how can we help?*

LAMA SING: This is a very excellent question.

When entities are unprepared in the sense that they have not been aware or have chosen to ignore the likelihood of death of the body and if, in such circumstances, you or others are present, there should be every effort made to acquaint the entity with their full and complete power of mind and spirit. They should be made to know that preconceived thoughts, dogmas, and attitudes, which have been embedded within them by their life, will restrict their progress and their awareness only to the limit that they are willing to accept.

There should be discussion, openly, of the unlimited nature of their being, because they are a creation of God. There should be discussions regarding the eternal nature of all things. Not just the soul of man, but everything continues to exist. It may change form, it may take on different brilliance, different density, but even the most minute organism or structure continues ... merging, separating, being in harmony, being at some discord, all these experiences.

There should be references made to the entity's ability to focus upon that which they believe in from their heart, to select from that which they have learned and been taught, in a sort of combined or summarial form, and to focus upon this image.

There should be good sounds, pleasant, happy voices. There should be color, light ... happiness! We know that this may seem foreign to some, but consider for a moment the ecstasy with which one greets a newborn babe, and then turn around completely and look at the lifetime of experiences that that child must face in the Earth plane, for example, at this very time. We find that in many instances this may be rather awesome, and you may wish to quickly tell the child to return from whence it came because of the tremendous effort that you might see ahead of this child.

Well death, then: a point of sadness, the loss of a comrade, a friend, a mate, a companion who has become endeared. But consider for a moment that their life's work has been completed and that they have engaged now in a moment of culmination of that entire lifetime; that they are preparing to step forward and to recognize a new facet of God; that they are preparing to receive guidance, loving companionship far beyond most entity's ability to imagine! Hold to this. If you must hold to thoughts of a meadow of flowers, beautiful structures, trees, colors, sound, whatever you can think of which promotes harmony and beauty within yourself, and then serve from that level of consciousness.

And lastly, but most importantly, do urge the entity to often be in joyous prayer; and to be forgiving of themselves and others. There are ceremonies, which will be spoken of in a few moments, which emphasize this most important part of departure from the Earth plane into other realms.

QUESTION 5: *How should we think of those who have passed on?*

LAMA SING: Think of them in much the same way as you did when they were in the Earth plane, for it would be this thought of love and kindness and familiarity which will suit them well. Do not think of them in terms of sadness, anger, remorse, betrayal, as so many do in their grief of their loss. Release them lovingly and with a prayer, and do this often.

QUESTION 6: *So our thoughts can then be helpful, or they can be detrimental?*

LAMA SING: Your thoughts can be detrimental or helpful. The choice is often made without the awareness of the effect upon the departed soul. Do you wish further comment on this?

Q 6-2: *Yes, I think we have to discuss, first of all, what thoughts, and in which way they are helpful. And after that we will move on to what thoughts, and in which way they are detrimental, as so many people have a definite problem with that and it is very hard to understand.*

First of all: helpful, what thoughts are helpful, which way?

LAMA SING: Search through your minds for the happiest experiences that you can recall between you and the departed entity. Think of the events, the moments, and the words which were exchanged which promoted happiness and harmony. Once this feeling is created, then release the actual words, or events, and hold the feelings. Then, think of the entity's name and then state a prayer similar to this:

Eternal God, we give to Thee now this most beloved

soul (state their name). We pray Thee now to guide, to counsel, as you often have while this soul was in the Earth plane. We ask humbly that you take them in loving kindness and warmth, as they shall always be held in our heart, and deliver them unto those purposes, and those kindred souls with whom they shall now serve in accord with Thy will. For this we thank Thee, ever, Father. Amen.

With such a prayer, you release them to their benefit and to God. And, incidentally, you assure practically, without exception, an open communicative line of communication of sorts between yourself and that soul.

QUESTION 7: *What is detrimental, and in which way?*

LAMA SING: Perhaps the most obstructive is that of bitterness, anger, hatred. It is much like attempting to travel in one of your automobiles on a busy highway in the dark of night in a dense fog. The soul cannot see where to go. Thus, the soul is often forced to turn back to whence it came. These souls are often identified as "bound to the Earth" by these thoughts, these attitudes. (Now this differs somewhat from souls who willingly bind themselves to the Earth plane out of carnal desires, habits or patterns which they are unable to break at the moment of death of the body).

You must ever pray, ever search within self, to find and to release such attitudes, such emotions. Just an increment behind these emotions lies perhaps one of the most difficult to understand (we will try to explain it), and that is the attitude of sorrow and tremendous love of those who are bereaved, left behind (so to say). This intense emotion, and this tremendous desire to have their loved one back, to hold them, is the actual creation of clouds, of fog, and of restraint to their forward progress.

There is some period of time wherein the soul, upon departure from the Earth, will linger generally within the realms of the Earth plane. At this time, other souls will come to join the newly arrived soul. They will, in essence, protect the soul from influences of souls, entities, who have chosen to remain close to the Earth out of their own desires. But they [the protecting souls] can remain in these realms, by your measurement, only certain lengths of time. Ultimately, they must return to their own level of consciousness and continue their functions. The exceptions to this are the Angelic Host, the Souls of Glory, the Prince of Peace and His Servants. Other souls, who are as joyous glad helpers, must ultimately return to their own levels.

So, then, you can see from this that if the period of bereavement and grief and abashed love is too long, too intense, the soul will be, in essence, held somewhat in realms close to the Earth plane, unable to continue, ultimately forced … Well, perhaps that's a poor choice of terms. For, again, there are great strengths which certain souls can build to move well beyond the Earth plane, and very rapidly so. However, these are moreover the exceptions, unfortunately. In general, the soul would be relatively close to the Earth plane, and would be dependent somewhat upon its own resources after a time. See?

QUESTION 8: *We have also seen lingering take place when a person is supposedly dying, or dead, or in a vegetative situation, where the person has not been allowed to completely go on. The body has not completely stopped living because of other entities loving them so much that they simply cannot release them. Would you help us with that?*

LAMA SING: In your prayers, just before the term, Amen, should be this phrase: And above all, O Father, Thy will, not mine, be done.

In other words:

I pray to Thee, Father, that Thee should hear this plea. I place now my will and my accord with Thee. Help Thou this soul now before me. If it be to the soul's purpose and in accord with Thy will, let the entity be healed. If this soul be needed in service elsewhere, in love, in kindness, and in the knowledge of eternal life through the Christ, I commit my will to Thine.

QUESTION 9: *What of those, Lama Sing, who are kept alive artificially with machinery? Where perhaps the mother would like to disconnect the machinery because the child has not really been there for two years, and yet, by the law of the country, we cannot do this type of thing. And we can see our child, let's say for instance, lying there for years, kept alive with a machine. If they are truly meant to go forward that way, how can we do this so that the machine can then be disconnected, and everything can go on?*

LAMA SING: Well, do recall that the body is the vehicle. And the thread, which binds the soul (or consciousness of the entity) to the vehicle or physical body, is very elastic, in that as one images in his mind a luminous filament which connects the soul consciousness, or total awareness, to that of the physical form which is defined, this can span dimensions incomprehensible by three-dimensional standards. Though the body is in all aspects alive and functioning to a limited extent, the soul is, in essence, well about its functions, its duties.

In the case of such an event, the soul could at any moment choose to return and awaken in that physical form sufficiently long enough to allow it to die a natural death. So the burden or choice, in truth, needn't be made at the Earth plane. The soul would make this from its total consciousness. In essence, the true question is whether or not to leave the plug plugged in or whether to remove it.

Remember the Master's teachings that, so as ye are in the land of mankind and you live within the laws of man, then there must be the collective change of these laws. But, lest thee offend thy neighbor and thy tribe, you must do honor to that which exists. If there is inadequacy in the governing of mankind then change these, but do not burden one friend, one neighbor, with such a decision … (a matter which urgently cries out for exploration).

Would there be a fault were the plug removed? We would not find that there should be fault here. Were you to remove the plug, the soul would at that moment make its final decision whether to re-enter or whether to terminate the relationship with that physical form. (We pray Thee, Father, guide these words that they be understood, and that they have been given through the Christ in accord with Thee.)

Each entity is responsible, to their ability, to give what they have to give to their brethren. That which goes beyond and is not of the natural, or of the etheric, blessings (and this is, in essence, a very complex matter), well, when this occurs there is a digression from the natural life force. It is very similar to initiating the creation of life. One does not command God that this or that shall be in existence because of my will but, rather, asks God to allow His will to be exercised through thee. Thus thee become a servant, an implement in God's vineyard.

God guides thee, as certainly as a rudder guides a vessel in the sea, if thee would only listen. If you would meditate and pray each day, God would guide thee, and you would know beyond doubt, beyond question, that this is God's will.

QUESTION 10: *Would you please discuss the phrase "death with dignity"—and this was perhaps what mom wanted for her mom, when she said, "Remove the tubes, and let her be."*

LAMA SING: The term is one which is extracted from a composite statement. However, "death with dignity" would be defined in this way by this gathering: Within the attitude and forbearance of one's continual life in consciousness, let this be allowed to be maintained throughout the moment of transition.

Death should no moreso be a violation of one's belief, in their consciousness than one would violate that continuity were the entity, as you call it, alive in the physical body. If an entity believed that they must be buried in the color black, you would not dispute it at the moment of their death. In other words, allow the continuation of their philosophy, their belief, their way of life, their attitude, to remain intact throughout the transition. See?

Q 10-2: *That reminds me of a beautiful story, of friends, where the mother was passing away and her daughter had always promised to sew her a long red velvet dress and she never got around to it. And so when the mother passed away, she had the material and said, "I will make that dress"—which she did—and had her mother buried in it. And now she is always able to see her mother beautifully dancing in her long, red velvet dress, which is what she always wanted to do.*

It is a continuity of love, an expression of love, which allowed the entity to more properly release her mother and was a very good action.

We recall the entity well.

QUESTION 11: *Why have many organized religions prepared special sacraments to follow in preparing for life hereafter?*

LAMA SING: There are several extractions from past activities which relate to this particular activity. All of them to be given would be too lengthy. These would be those which you would be familiar with:

Atlantean

During the Atlantean period of time it was recognized that an entity was a visitor within the body and within the Earth plane. During the time which preceded this it, was very clear and very well known, but you are less aware of those times. So in the Atlantean, the recognition that, often, entities would not be aware of their death, would not be aware of their departure, and there would be a series of ceremonies which would be performed, firstly, to help the entity, to guide them by joining spiritual energies into a common pool, so to say, and directing this for the entity's growth and for their journey.

American Indian

Others would find that there might have been some attitude, some emotion, which could restrict the departed soul's advancement. This particular aspect was carried over into the North American Indian tribal customs, wherein an entity was placed upon a pyre, or platform, which was elevated. And those who knew the entity, and who had emotional and mental holds upon the entity's spirit, were required to seat themselves around his body, until they were able to release all of these bonds, these holds upon the entity. Thus their cherished belongings were consumed in the ultimate fire with the entity so as not to hold the entity by the possession of an axe, an implement, a bow, feathers, whatsoever the item was, thereby helping to release themselves completely from the Earth.

Egyptian

Throughout the evolution (as it is called) of mankind's consciousness, this was altered somewhat. The realization that they could help departed souls by their conscious efforts (on the part of those in the Earth plane, that is) was carried through from the Atlantean. in the Egyptian it was gradually altered from a time wherein a ceremony, sacraments, were preformed to tell the entity that he was released, that he was free from all burden, and to thank him or her for their participation.

Tibetan

Off to the side, in the Tibetan, very significantly spiritual ceremonies were performed to help all souls who had recently departed, not just those whom they knew of but any other souls who might be having difficulty in transition. It was a regular ceremony, a sort of daily funeral, if you will.

Early Christian

The sacraments then evolved as a part of the Egyptian into the Coptic, the Celts, into the times of the Master's own presence, wherein He spoke to them and said: Let My dignity remain with Me throughout. And He asked them to leave His body intact, only to the spiritual significance and ceremony, that He would hold this dignity unto God and that He would return intact. (The Egyptians, as you know, varied this somewhat.)

American

In North America, it became a part of a later culture to hold this as a period of bereavement, a period of salvation. Only a part of it became recitation of the entity's achievement. That portion was intended to make the soul aware of its life, if there was a difficulty at that time, on the individual soul's part. It's very involved and a very complex mechanism, by which it has evolved to your present time.

QUESTION 12: *Is the mental ingraining of special death rites beneficial or harmful, during or after the transition period? And if it slows one's transition, please explain.*

LAMA SING: On the basis of which the question is asked, it is, in the dogmatic sense, harmful, if it is believed that this is the only way to reach God. It would not have an effect to an entity who knows that God is not limited and thus would by no means reject an entity simply because of a ritual.

QUESTION 13: *Lama Sing, in having a funeral or that type of thing, does the person involved [whom the funeral is for] stay around, or stay close by until after the funeral rites are done for all those who care about that soul? Or are they long gone, and it is just for us on the Earth plane?*

LAMA SING: This varies, dependent upon the soul's purposes and the works which the soul was involved in. There is no procedural, step-by-step activity. It is a matter of choice.

QUESTION 14: *Please discuss the last rites performed by the Catholic Church. When and where did this practice originate? Other than the mind believing so, does it actually help in transition?*

LAMA SING: For those who believe it, it certainly does. We have seen some who wait for long periods of time to receive what you call certain ceremonies, which they feel are essential. And unfortunately, in some cases, these souls are recalling a ritual which took place several lifetimes previous to the present departure. They still haven't released it. In such cases they are helped by other souls. The Catholic religion has many aspects of their last rites which are beautiful and very meaningful. They have been somewhat altered over the years, and the belief, the purpose here, is the creation of spiritual and mental forms.

The symbology of the anointing of the head is the transference of energies through the pineal, pituitary centers. The soul has emerged, essentially, at the abdominal region, and the method of communication is always thought to be at the crown chakra, or the head. And the symbol placed here, along with prayer and thought, the anointing, is to make the soul conscious of its oneness with God. And so the ceremony became one which was believed to be, then, essential to departure, and essential to assurance of acceptance into the Kingdom of God.

The confession, or relieving of one's guilt, is a matter which came from, in actuality, the Atlanteans, but was practiced in early Egyptian and transferred through the Mohabites into the Hebraic as a form of release of one's own blocks or obstructions between self and God. And it was earlier practiced in the Atlantean as a group activity. Thus it became sacred, and was practiced only between those who were the entities dying, and those who were selected to be worthy to pass judgment and to forgive in God's name. (That may be rather poorly given to you. We trust it's of some value.)

QUESTION 15: *If last rites are of important benefit, then what about those to whom such rites are not given? Is their transition more difficult?*

LAMA SING: Yes, to those who believe they must have this for departure and for acceptance into the Kingdom of God. Ultimately, they are helped in this regard by other loving souls. In actuality, the sacraments, or the last rites, are not essential to acceptance in the Kingdom of God.

We know that some who hear this would have many

thoughts and words to speak. We ask these to consider this for a moment: Do you wish to create, and to live, a lifetime referring to a God so limited that He would not accept one of His children because of a ceremony? Or do you prefer to recognize God as totally and completely without limitation, full well knowledgeable of your every thought, your every intent, your past, your present, and future; and to recognize that if you have chosen a time of departure which does not afford a ceremony that your heart, mind, and your soul are pure in a certain thought and attitude?

We do not wish to offend. We only speak the truth as it is given here. The sacramental rites are very beautiful and they serve good purpose, if they are thought of in the manner which we have described.

QUESTION 16: *What should be the ultimate way to allow someone to pass over, for the benefit of their soul and them, and the benefit of those here? What would be the ultimate funeral, let us say?*

LAMA SING: How has the entity believed during their lifetime?

If they have believed in a certain way, then this is the way that you should honor that entity, by giving them their dignity of continuity. And if you have a belief which is not limited to ceremony, not limited to rote or dogma, then your final mechanism should honor that.

If an entity loved the meadows, the forest, or the glen, then gather in the places the entity loved most. And, indeed, where possible, in those areas where the entity frequented most. And smile, and remember, and hold happily in your hearts and in your prayers, the wonders of their presence, giving thanks to God, and allowing them to go about their work in God's name (as previously given). See?

QUESTION 17: *What about the actual body itself? Should it perhaps be buried at the place they most frequented? Or (cre-*

mated, if they would like it so)... the ashes cast about at the place they most frequently enjoyed?

LAMA SING: We would find that most entities have a preference and we would honor this were we in the Earth plane. The question, as it is asked from here, would receive a very strong comment towards the reducing of the body to its basic form and allowing it to become, thusly, in harmony with the surroundings in which it has best found its joy, its harmony. To make this clear: The action of cremation and the dispersing of the resulting final form of the physical body should be placed in those areas of the entity's own choosing. Some will not find this method acceptable; then their wishes should, by all means, be honored. See?

Q 17-2: *Is that how we got the statement, "ashes to ashes, dust to dust?" And what of scattering the ashes on water?*

LAMA SING: It is, in essence, the same, yes. We would find this to be one of the best of all choices, for the waters of thy land are in harmony with the elements, save in those areas where man has disrupted them, and they continue to re-purify themselves regardless of the presence of any other forces. Thus your presences, whether it be in ash or even in the physical body, in or near the waters, will always be purifying.

QUESTION 18: *Please discuss what actually happens to those who seem to have died--after-death experiences--and then returned to life. Why are they permitted this experience?*

LAMA SING: In most cases the entities chose to return to the Earth plane, because they could further their soul's growth in some manner or another. See?

Q 18-2: Is it also perhaps in many times--let's say for instance, a life of drunkenness--an accident and being saved from that, completely turning their lives around at that time. Is it perhaps to change their route?

LAMA SING: Oh, yes. But understand this, the soul has no intention at any time in such a case of the body ever dying! This was merely done to awaken it to the fact that it was wasting the lifetime.

This often happens in other ways as well, but there is no intention of the soul to release that body. It merely appears so on the Earth plane.

QUESTION 19: *Are most of us conscious of the transition as it is taking place, or are we simply awakened to find a transition has already been made?*

LAMA SING: Oh, yes. But understand this, the soul has no intention at any time in such a case of the body ever dying! This was merely done to awaken it to the fact that it was wasting the lifetime. This often happens in other ways as well, but there is no intention of the soul to release that body. It merely appears so on the Earth plane.

You will awaken, then, a bit confused, out of reference. Well, occasionally an entity will make the transition, as it is called, with a similar reaction.

Some souls are able to maintain full consciousness at the level of their being during the transition. But even then we find that most here would comment that their experiences have always been to suddenly realize that that experience had come to a conclusion.

And it's very pleasant, as though a fresh breeze were to suddenly sweep across your body, and it would be fragrant and light and cleansing. It's an extremely pleasant experience! All the entities here concur in that.

QUESTION 20: *One time [during a reading] when we contacted a deceased person, or one on your side, they stated, "Yes he is here, playing checkers and arguing with comrades that have passed on before him that he has not passed on. He always played checkers on the Earth plane, he is still playing checkers here. And he continues to argue that he isn't dead, that he is still on the Earth plane." Why does that take place?*

LAMA SING: Well, it may seem humorous to you and, indeed, perhaps it is. It's just as we gave. "So as you believe …" you see. This phrase cannot be emphasized too frequently. Your beliefs, your attitudes, and your thoughts build, not just in the sense of the physical lifetime but well beyond.

This entity is still functioning under the auspices of his Earth plane's thoughts and attitudes. And since it's his choice, his comrades are lovingly participating with him, occasionally mentioning to him that, "After all, dear friend, you are dead, you know. You don't exist in that form any longer."

And the entity may, at one point, suddenly realize what they are saying and not pass it off. Then the entire environment will change, and he will assume a greater consciousness and go on. See?

QUESTION 21: *Please outline the movement of consciousness during the period of transition, such as awareness of:*

a. Out-of-Body

b. Existing in other dimensions

c. Movement to Arcturus.

LAMA SING: We are unclear in some portions of that question. It presupposes certain activities which are not either common nor, in essence, the standard for souls making transition. Restate the question please.

a. Out-of-Body awareness

LAMA SING: The entity is fully aware at the moment of transition, of their departure from the physical body. That is to say, that they are fully conscious of themselves and yet are no longer in their physical bodies. But this is not necessarily limited to the moment of departure or the action of death. This can occur throughout the lifetime and frequently does. Also, an entity is conscious as being out of the body, so to say, but is neither limited by that fact nor necessarily concerned regarding it. Yet others might find that they do not believe they have left the body. So, in either case, the question is not one that needs to be concerned over from that aspect. (Please forgive us.)

b. Existing in other dimensions

LAMA SING: You must recognize that you exist in all dimensions simultaneously. You must further recognize that you are limited to this recognition only by the limitations which you impose upon self and God. Thus, to the limit of your ability to accept the fact that God is unlimited, so do thee recognize then that you are, indeed, in a realm different from the one you just departed, yet you still exist in all realms. The simultaneity of a soul's existence is too complex a matter for the Earth plane to comprehend at this time. Even though it has been given by certain channels in the Earth plane, we do find that this matter is, for the most part, overwhelming. We ask your indulgence and your patience for that particular topic.

c. Movement to Arcturus

Such movement that is to Arcturus is generally limited to those souls who have reached their consciousness so as to recognize Arcturus as a realm of existence as just given.Arcturus is (as we have given previously) a focal point, a sort of axial point, from which a soul enters a completely different spectrum of realms where existence is multidimensional, as where consciousness is in harmony with these multiple dimensions. The functions here are those which are very closely aligned to the Christ, and it is often thought of to be the throne of the Christ spirit. Thus, one would not approach the Master until they are worthy within themselves … and that means, simply, willing to accept.

CONDUCTOR: *We have no further questions at this time. I think we have covered many, many aspects. Are there any that need further clarification? Or are there any at this time that we are overlooking that are important for people to be aware of in this lecture?*

CLOSING COMMENTS

Be aware of this: that "so as ye sow, thusly shall thee reap." The Master has spoken these words and they have been echoed in most religions, beliefs and dogmas, most societies, and in individual minds and hearts.

Universal Law, as it is called, applies in this way: that so as there is a thought which is manifested, this thought must be honored. These are seeds; the honoring of the thought is the harvesting. Thus your own thoughts will build because you must honor them, you must give them substance.

In dealing with mass-mind thought, you have an aggregate of thoughts and attitudes. Learning to live with this aggregate is a part of preparing for departure from the body.

You must reflect, daily, upon the very real fact that you exist because God has created thee; that you exist to function, to experience and to realize that you have never once left God; that at this very moment you are, in essence, as much with God as you were in the moment of your creation. How can this be? What is thought, then? Thought is the mechanism, the distance, each of you have built, literally built, between you and God. Spend as much time of your present life's experience lovingly realizing that you have but to ask in His name and so shall it be given unto thee. In the believing, so it is done.

We have had a great joy to have been with thee once again, dear friends. And we thank all of those present in this and other realms, for their loving kindness. We again pray that these words and thoughts have reached your heart, in the openness and love with which they have been given.

We ask that the spirit of the Christ, which is as to say that the filament which binds your souls to ours and all souls, be with thee. Thank Thee, Father, and thee, dear friends. Fare thee well.

Reading Three:

Suicide

And Its Spiritual Implications

This reading was given January 16, 1996.

—

AL MINER/CHANNEL: This reading is a request for a topical research reading on the topic of suicide. I want to thank my two very dear friends in Arizona for coming up with this request and also the considerable work that they put into developing the questions.

As always, we submit these questions to You, Father, asking as we do that You would guide us to that information that You would know to be the best for us now and in the future.

So, let me read what has been written:

QUESTIONS

Dear Al and Unseen Friends: Maybe you can shed some light on this subject. In some of Lobsang Rampa's books, there's one that deals exclusively with this topic. He stated that a suicide is a suicide and will be dealt with as such, in that you shortened your contractual life span and, in essence, cheated your soul of the experience. You would therefore be re-activated quickly—go back to Earth, and more or less fulfill your contract or intent.

To those unfamiliar with Rampa, he is, was, a highly educated Tibetan Lama who, after a very serious illness, took over another body – a walk-in, so to speak – to fulfill a job: to write several books (which are available in metaphysical book stores), which really brings us to our first question.

1. As in the incident described by Rampa in his book, the person who offered his body as the vehicle for this cause had no desire, no will, to live any more. Was or is this a form of suicide?

2. What constitutes a suicide? Are there different degrees of suicide that are dealt with more "severely" than others?

3. Is there a soul awareness that its vehicle (physical body) will experience suicide during the course of a certain lifetime so that the suicide is contractual, so to speak?

4. Are there people who are prone to suicide by virtue of heredity?

5. On a professional level, are there times when one should or should not interfere or prevent suicide? How does one help a person who is suicidal? Any suggestions? (I guess we could look at that from either perspective, dependent upon your answer to number 5.)

6. An entity who chooses not to follow the doctor's advice and consequently shortening his life, is that considered a suicidal scenario? (In other words, are they, in effect, committing suicide by not following medical advice, on some level?)

When such an individual is married, could there also be the soul intent of his or her mate involved? Perhaps wanting to find out how the surviving mate would handle this situation could play a part in their attitude about continuing on with life. Your comments, please.

7. In the book, Plato's "Republic", we find Aristotle condemned to death and then chose hemlock, thereby cheating his executioner. Was or is that sort of thing the same as a traditional suicide?

8. A person at a "rational" moment, choosing suicide because of severe health problems so as not to burden their spouses and family, material or otherwise. What is your perspective on something such as that? That certainly seems to gray the traditional definition of suicide, when the greatest thought of the severely ill person is to avoid burdening their spouse or family, or is that a cop-out?

9. What about those who are comatose, and patients who are on artificial life support systems, where there is absolutely no hope in sight, where, in such cases communication does not exist between patient and family any more?

10. Please give us your comments on assisted suicide,

like the work Dr. Kevorkian is doing. It is considered legal in some states. We seem to be more compassionate toward our domesticated animals in putting them to sleep when they can longer able be helped medically. Where, on the opposite side of the coin, terminally ill patients receiving less than adequate medicine to relieve their pain, for fear they might become addicted to the medication.

11. Any suggestions on how to help the family members of suicides after the fact?

12. In the fortress Masada, where the Israelites were not able to withstand the Roman siege any more, and instead of surrendering it was decided to commit mass suicide, did all these entities choose this group suicide on the soul level, or was it spontaneous, or cosmic, in a sense? Was there a conscious aware-ness of the consequences thereof?

13. And, lastly, are there entities who terminate their life knowing there would be no future in the incarnation?

I think that's certainly sufficient questions and so, again, Father, we humbly request that you would guide us to that information that you know would be most helpful in all respects on this topic. And as always, we pray this of you, Father, in the name of the Master, the Christ. And we thank you, Father, for this and the many other blessings that you give us each and every day. Amen.

OPENING COMMENTS & ANSWERS

LAMA SING: Yes, we have the Channel then and, as well, those references which apply to the topic and those of the questions as are presented just above.

In considering the overall topic of suicide, it is perhaps of value to consider first of all: What is life?

We do not intend that that should sound hollow or empty

or too greatly philosophical, but the fact remains that life itself is eternal. And the current or any such sojourn in the Earth called life is, as we believe you would agree, quite brief, even if only comparatively analyzed on the linear scale of time from the geological viewpoint. Neither is it our intent by any comments that shall follow to imply license (so to say) to violate those laws, tenets and such, as are held sacred, important or, at the very least, worthy of being upheld in the Earth plane.

The point is simply this: that we are attempting to convey here (as we believe is the purest aspect of the intent by the inquirers), the spiritual implication to the action of deliberately ending one's life in physical body on the Earth.

Giving Over One's Body to a "Walk-in"

In the first question as is indicated by the precursive commentary (certainly of considerable value) when an entity relegates their opportunity for growth, for advancement, and other such in the Earth plane, and is willing in that sense to allow their life to end and another to enter in, this becomes, according to the term *walk-in*, quite a profound question, particularly as relates to its relevance to the topic *Suicide.*

And so, to avoid meandering on our part here, suffice to state that we would categorize this in the group of commentaries that shall follow, for the intent is basically the same. The only thing missing in this circumstance is the actual action of doing something deliberately to terminate the physical life.

In All Things, Consider the Intent

What constitutes, then, a suicide (and that appropriately follows the first question). It is, first and foremost, in all things that any entity is about, a*ny* works, the *intent* that is so very important in all these things. For as we have oft given here in past (and as clearly has been given often elsewhere), one's intent carries a profound spiritual connotation, if not a literal connotation in the Earth plane. There are instances in the Earth wherein the intent does not dull the result, where the intent might not be sufficient justification for what transpires, regardless of how well-intended that intent was. But in the spiritual aspect of the intent, this is very important.

So, in the suicide the intent is one, perhaps, of frustration, of a sense of hopelessness, a sense of failure, a sense of sadness, and any other such emotional descriptions that are certainly relevant in the Earth. What we could point to immediately after having stated those comments is that there must be, then, a lack of a goal, an intent, a spiritual ideal. And this underscores (again, as so often given in past) the importance of *having* an ideal, purpose, and goal.

What Is Suicide

But what is a suicide? It is the removal of opportunity. It is the calling to an end, deliberately, of opportunities that the soul has previously consented to. It is the action of terminating, not only one's own individual opportunities, but also the potential for the opportunities of interaction on the part of others with whom the suicide … we'll use the term *victim*, might have interacted. This, of course, raises many other subsets of questions, we should think, certainly of considerable validity in this topic. It is entirely possible that we shall only (as you call it) scratch the surface of the topic, but we shall do the best that we can in the time available here.

The Victim Chose the Conditions

Considering the suicide, consider this, as well: The conditions of the life in which the suicide is being considered are not idle. In other words, they simply cannot be cast aside casually. They are important. Why are they important? Because that soul has *chosen them.* That soul, the potential suicide victim, has carefully evaluated, counseled, and extended considerable effort to prepare for the best of all opportunities for their own growth and (again, as just indicated above) to contribute the opportunity for others to grow as well, those who may or may not become a part of that soul's interaction in that life in the Earth.

Now, we stated "may or may not" because there are choices all along the path. Each incarnation has many branches off the main trunk, which could be identified as the primary life movement. And as you know, these decisions, whether you consider them good or bad, do determine certain interactions or the absence thereof. But in spite of that, or perhaps because of it, the soul reaches a point at that time of suicide crisis (as it could be called) of making the greatest progress.

Attempts at "Heavenly" Intervention

Consider that in light of the intent of the subject (the one who is suicidal), if an entity is considering suicide and if that entity is, paradoxically, standing before or at the threshold of profound spiritual opportunities for growth. How can this be? Why isn't there some intervention, you might think, that would prevent the soul from falling prey to the emotional, the blinding pain of the current event, and help them to temper the pain, that they can see through it with greater sight and wisdom?

The answer to this is, quite straightforwardly, this is very often done ...very, very often. Were it not, your suicide rate per capita would be substantially higher than it is at present. In those instances where it appears not to have been given (in other words, help to be given, strength to be offered, and so on and so forth) those entities in most instances, generally speaking, would not hear, would not listen, could not be reached, so to say. Even in these, there are instances where you will find they were ineffectual in their attempt and woke up disappointed, perhaps in an emergency room, whereupon they were given treatment and counseling and such, and returned to resume their life.

Suicide Other Than Termination of Physical Life

So what constitutes a suicide? Well, the questions presented above primarily focus upon the termination of the physical life, the death of the body. What about the suicides wherein the body does not die? What about those entities who commit suicide when they are presented with an opportunity for change? What about those who succumb to limitation, even though they know inwardly that they could expend more energy, more effort, more deliberation, and succeed? What about those who bury self, somewhat suicidally, in the habits and thinking of the past?

So, you see, there are variations upon this topic that are broad in their scope. There are variants within each day's life in the Earth that approach, if not embrace, the concept of suicide. There are those entities who perform actions (perhaps sometimes only subtly conscious of them, but other times almost deliberately) in the full knowledge that those actions will eventually culminate in their death, the death of their physical body. And there are those actions that will certainly short-circuit the potential for the accomplishment of the greatest of all growth in that lifetime.

Then, is the signet of suicide, so to say, placed only upon that group (comparatively small, you see) who actually perform an action that causes the termination of their physical life? The answer to that is, no. There are those actions, those misdeeds, or opportunities missed by deliberate intent, that place such entities in the same category of treatment as those who actually commit the suicidal action. See?

Degrees of Suicide

So there are different degrees and, though we would not use the term *severity* or such (with a note of loving humor), they are treated with the same respect and concern and love, for we do not consider it a punishment or anything harsh or that sort to provide for a suicide victim to re-enter the Earth rapidly. That is an action of profound love. It is an enactment of God's Universal Laws in the most profound sense of same.

When you look to your friends, your neighbors, your family, your associates, and you see them repeating the same limiting thought over and over again, you might also (because you have some knowledge of such things) say to yourself, "Well, they'll have to meet that in another life. They'll have to choose a lifetime of opportunity for growth again and again, until they have learned to balance with same." True? So, to a subtle extent, they are destroying, if you will, their opportunity for growth. Yes, it is true, that could be considered quite passive when compared to the action of suicide, but it is, nonetheless, the death of the opportunity. But so long as their life pattern continues, there is always the opportunity that these souls can be reached … that a teacher, a worker, or a channel, can come before them and awaken them. Perhaps even you, dear friends.

Again, the point is simply this: Do not base all evaluation and/or judgment of what constitutes a suicide based upon purely the suicidal action.

Fear and Faith in the Suicidal Intent

Fear is often the triggering mechanism that predicates the suicidal intent, as strange as that might sound—fear of movement, fear of the unknown, fear of the loss of something that was held dear, or fear of being limited, and on and on. So the counterpoint to fear, of course, is obviously faith.

We could conclude, then, based on that little analogy or example, that one of the best ways to reach someone who is demonstrating suicidal tendencies is to fill them with faith, to inspire them with hope, to be the example that… no matter what, God always provides a path to transcend the darkest times, to overcome the most painful challenge or limitation. See?

How the Time of "Re-Entry" Is Determined

Dependent upon what we could call … (searching for a descriptive term, a moment please). Very well. Dependent upon what we might call the *growth potential quotient* … In other words, let us presume for a moment that we have nine suicide victims (as you call them) who have recently crossed over into these and other realms. And of these nine, we might assess that three of the entities were in the midst of lifetimes which had a 70 percent *growth potential*. In other words, they could have gained 70 percent greater spiritual enlightenment had they not concluded that lifetime than where they were when they started, and of course probably where they are still, right now, here in these realms. The other seven might have varying lesser percentiles, and so their re-entry would be ranked behind the first three, proportionately speaking.

Now, you must understand that we are using this example and the quotient for illustrative purposes. It is not dealt with coldly or calculatively. It is dealt with in an attitude of complete love, understanding, forgiveness, and, of course, with the full complement of knowledge, intimately, of each of these souls … their past, their present, and the potential for their future. And because of the movement of the Earth, the mind set, the mass-mind thought, the conditions, et cetera, of the three who are placed at the forefront for re-entry into the Earth, conditions which are prevalent at that time may well be those which are so very suitable, so very conducive to the attainment of this spiritual lesson or lessons, that they will truly be given what you would consider to be a very swift opportunity for return.

This carries with it certain other factors that might be worthy of note here, and so, we'll mention them just briefly. Understanding that the first incarnation, which was voluntarily terminated by the entity or entities, was carefully planned, carefully thought out, so to say. The interactions, the associations, the soul groups, and so forth all were carefully and lovingly considered, and perhaps considered over a span of Earth time that might measure from many years to hundreds of years or greater. But, in the case of these first three entities, it is entirely possible for one or more of them to re-enter in a matter of days. Yes, that was our intent, *days*.

Now, you measure time differently than we here. We can move in a parallel to your time and accomplish the effect of what you would measure to be many Earth years. So the fact that only three Earth days might transpire and a suicide victim is already on their way, returning to a new body and so forth, is of no significant worthy note here. But from your perspective, we have no doubt it will seem remarkable in its rapidity.

The point is simply this: Those circumstances as we indicated were carefully chosen. They are important to all three of these entities and, indeed, to varying degrees, to the other seven. If those specific circumstances are not critical, then, of course, this can be a variable taken into consideration. But for the most part, all of these entities, the nine or ten (as we've done our mathematics here) would return very quickly. They would return in priority over most all other souls. See?

So the bottom line (with a note of loving humor) for our dear colleague, who is the primary inquirer here, is that it's a rapid turn-around. If you leave by your own hand, you'll return almost immediately … comparatively speaking, a handful of Earth days.

A Life To Which the Suicide Victim Might Return

Generally, there will not be, as we would consider it here, the better circumstances on the next re-entry as there were in the former. The reason for that is not a punishment, it is the lack of what we'll call spiritual opportunity, and the soul of the suicide victim has much to do with this. In other words, it's difficult to awaken fully some of these entities, and so they are returned still feeling some of the same self-guilt, some of the same emotion, et cetera, as they did just before they left the Earth and, therefore, it might be difficult to give them the same or better circumstances of their just-previous life.

In fact, sometimes these souls will not accept the same equivalent of their just-previous life, but insist on punishing themselves and may, indeed, be re-born into the Earth to live only a short span of time again and again, perhaps succumbing to famine or pestilence in what you call one of your third-world countries, or to be the victim of some event as a dis-ease or what you call war and those things, believing that so doing contributes to the mass-mind consciousness, spiritually speaking, by being the willing example of the fruits of such limited thinking, of the by-product of hatred and all that sort. We must concur, then, that such an action on the part of a suicide victim is a benevolent act, and it does contribute to them in the spiritual sense. But it is, you see, their choice and not a dictum from here, not a punishment.

Were we, in this group now communicating, given the opportunity, we would seek to provide them with greater comfort and assurance. In effect, perhaps, a little easier lesson than they had originally chosen because, after all, they couldn't deal with it, could they? But again, the bottom line is, take a shortcut out of the Earth and you'll have the fast lane back (humorously given) … Very fast.

There are instances wherein the soul might preview their life which is pending and note that there will be severe challenges. But at the time of the review it is very rare for an entity to consider that, "Oh, I might at this point not be able to make it, and take my own life." We don't have any records before us at the moment that indicate that a soul has so done. However, that does not mean that it is not possible.

Suicidal Tendencies as Heredity

If you consider mass-mind thinking and such to be a part of the term *heredity* then, yes, there are persons prone to suicide by such factors. But generally speaking, we do not find that the pure biological or genetic factors are blueprints for suicide, so to say.

There are genetic characteristics, as we are told here, that enable entities to have stronger neurological systems and such that can produce strengthening emotional electrochemical production that enable entities to have greater or lesser states of ease under pressure, challenge, during times of sadness and/or loss or failure or such, and these are widely known in the medical community. But beyond the production of such as endorphins and similar things such as this, and the biochemical factors that are a part of the genetic make-up, it is moreso the thinking, the attitude, the structure of the nurturing of the entity while in the womb and after birth and through childhood that would be looked at in askance as far as the true hereditary factors that can contribute to suicidal attitude. See?

Intervention

Regarding the question dealing with the intervention of one who is potentially suicidal, we'll answer this carefully in this way: You are responsible for your actions. You are also responsible for your lack thereof.

If you have knowledge that a flame can burn a child, and you do not tell them and they are burned, do you feel that you have done a right thing or a wrong thing? After all, you have actually done nothing. (Well, certainly we know the answer that you will give.)

If you see an entity walking down a sidewalk in a busy street, and you have just passed an open (as you call them) manhole cover and you see that the entity is gazing in a storefront, looking at the advertisements and such, you could do nothing and let them fall into the manhole opening. But you'll probably grab their arm and point to the open manhole.

So the question becomes a rather insignificant, if not moot, point, does it not? If you know of someone who is in such a state, you are the keeper of your brethren. So, as you have the knowledge and the power, and you use it not, then you will place upon yourself some debt, some karmic burden. Not a punishment. Perhaps a guilt in your mind, but in truth a missed opportunity. Could you not counter this in a question such as: "Perhaps the only reason that entity reached the suicidal point is to inspire me to become more spiritual, more loving, more giving … to reach out and to save a brother, a sister."

Attempted Intervention Not Heeded

You are responsible for your actions to the extent that you offer them, that you make the effort, that you extend the prayer, the comment, the embrace. If the entity does not accept it, that is not your responsibility, for Universal Law states clearly that each entity's right of Free Will is sacred.

For those who have incurred suicide in their family, in their friendships, among their associates, use the most powerful tool that you have to help the entity who has recently crossed over: the continuous flow of loving light through prayer, the prayer of preservation that they can reach the highest and best in the spiritual light of God, that they will hear and receive guidance from God's good workers, his Angelic Host, and all those other souls who serve humbly in His name. (More can be given on this, in terms of the other ramifications of such, so as you wish it.)

Intentional versus Unintentional Suicide

If an entity is told, "Do not do this or that any longer, or it will cause your premature departure from the Earth" or an entity, conversely, is told, "You must do this or that or your body will fail you, and your departure from this lifetime will be earlier than it need be," and, similarly, with medication and such, on and on, you could certainly consider that a degree of suicidal intent, could you not? But the question still remains: Has this caused the failure of the opportunity? The opportunity is not measured here nor by the soul in terms of time, as you call it such. (And, again, we point to our comments at the onset so as not to imply license, so to say, to the abandon of what you know to be right or correct, but only to respond to the question in a spirit of truth, as it has been requested of us.)

So, if you know a continuation along a certain path of action or inaction is going to cause you a shorter life than you might otherwise have, then, if you are spiritually enlightened, you'll realize not to put off too long those things that are important. For if you do this intentionally (and there is that word again, intent) to avoid spiritual growth or the resolution of those things that thou knoweth must be met, then this raises you, categorically speaking, higher towards the highest mark or highest indicator or level, which is, of course, the intentional suicide or termination of the body's life. So it's a gradient factor, indeed. See? But if the intent is not for the avoidance of those things needed, those lessons which are important for the growth, but rather (as is in most cases) the nature, simply habit or ... How do you call this in the Earth? The belief that tomorrow is the better day to follow the suggestion or take that path or to eliminate this certain unproductive diet, et cetera, then you see the gradient factor here.

Now, remembering, of course, that for those who can attain a spiritual oneness (in other words, claim their heritage to greater and greater degrees) such matters are not relevant, for the spirit is the power that gives life, not the food or lack of it, not the habits, the exercise, and all that sort but the spirit. But when the spiritual light and heritage are not claimed, then the body is relegated to exist on those things temporal, those things which are of the Earth. Spirit is the source of all the body's needs (as, perhaps, difficult as that might seem for many entities to believe). What you take into your body is what? A handful of very basic compounds, chemically speaking, in the Earth plane. And yet, it is believed that these mere elements in the Earth give life. Spirit gives the life!

The body becomes the extension of the spirit, and the body uses those elements as the materials from which it builds. But the pattern is spiritual. The life is the spirit. Well… forgive the digression here, but it is relevant.

The Question of Aristotle's Suicide

We'll move to the question regarding Aristotle (with a note of loving humor) … a rather challenging lad, to say the least. It's difficult to categorize this entity, for, as he is historically portrayed, he's not typical.

The choice to end one's life with the certainty of mere hours later having someone else end it for you seems not to be a question of whether or not this is suicide, but rather has the life been lived to this point according to that life's pattern and ideal? With an entity such as Aristotle, there can be little or no question of this. He considered his right to be free, his right for individual thinking, individual action, to be the same as *oneness with God*. And therefore, his intent by this action is to prevent the last opportunity for another to control or dominate his God-given rights, his spirit, his freedom and so he chose this path as a final statement.

It was not to escape the life, but as a statement. There was no cowardice here. There was no lack of willingness to pursue life's challenges and opportunities. To the contrary, this soul is clearly willing, (with a note of loving humor) if not vigorously so. Certainly, the outward aspects are suicidal, but what is the *intent*? To end the life? No, but to make an eternal statement, that no power greater than God is held sacred within his intent, his belief. And he would rather, by his own choice, return to be one with God than to give any power to those who would seek to usurp, to deny, to withhold power, to dominate, to sequester the beauty of each individual soul.

Sparing a Loved One Hardship

Regarding, now, with another look back at the entity who chooses not to follow the white-coated gentleman's procedure or prescriptions, and comparing this to the just-given narrative. There are similarities: Let us say, where there is a terminally ill entity who cannot raise the spiritual acceptance level to be healed or to heal themselves; or has chosen such knowingly as a pathway prior to entering into this physical body, realizing that this would provide multiple opportunities not only for his family, perhaps his mate, but for the world in general, the medical community, the researchers, and on and on … to add himself or herself to the statistics, urging more research, more discovery, the consideration of alternatives, and on and on. (Very complex, the interactive, interwoven scenario, see?) But focusing this, for the sake of your question, upon the family and perhaps the mate, we would not consider that action, with its intent of love and benevolence to the surviving family, to be one categorically and clinically defined as a suicide.

When the belief is there can be no more contribution, when the belief is that all options, all alternatives as they are known to the entity have been explored and it seems self-evident that to perpetuate the existence means that this will impose tremendous hardships upon the mate or family, you could not categorize that with the one who gives up or abandons the opportunity without searching, without trying, without attempting to re-instill hope, without looking for some way to be of service. The suicide victim, we'll presume for the moment, has a reasonably healthy, whole body (that would not always be the case, but use it for this reference), as opposed to the terminally ill patient who perhaps cannot even care for himself or herself any longer. There is, from the spiritual perspective here, only a very dim comparison. See?

Those Who Can't Communicate Their Desires

It is difficult to comment in the broad or general sense regarding the comatose or such entities who cannot communicate regarding the continuity of their life, but we'll do our best here to give you some examples:

Very often, entities who are in what you'd call a comatose state have, during those times of being absent from the Earth or perhaps a singular prolonged absence already (as you call it, *on the other side*) in these realms, in some instances they have already reviewed their life and yet their body is still being kept alive in the Earth. In some instances, the entities are given the opportunity to return, providing that there is work that can be done for themselves or for others, or a contribution that can be made. In those instances, categorically speaking, you will find that the entity will awaken, having had what's called an NDE, or Near Death Experience.

In other instances, it will be considered a miracle; that all hope was given up except for perhaps a handful of entities, friends, family, and such, who maintained a perpetual vigil … speaking to, praying for, and being with the comatose entity as though the entity were not comatose, laughing, sharing, playing favorite music, and so forth … such can be powerful enough to heal any dis-ease, to correct and/or mend even the most serious injury, where the practitioners might know of no way to so do.

Faith. Remember? We gave it above. Faith dispels fear. Fear is almost always a part of the force which motivates the suicidal intent, which makes easier the transition from the Earth, even in such as the comatose, presuming, now, the comatose condition is not self-inflicted. (Even in those cases, this is sometimes correct as well.))

Dr. Kevorkian and Assisted Suicide

It is very difficult to comment broadly, in other words, without speaking about each individual assisted suicide by this entity. In some instances, we find that his works or assisted suicides were not by chance, but were a part of what we'll call a very elaborate karmic interaction, coursing over many thousands of Earth years. And since we haven't his permission or request before us to discuss this, we cannot violate God's Law and do so. But we can state that in a number of these, there were karmic interactions from the past involved here. In the several that were not karmically interacted to past lives between the assisted suicide victim and the assistor, the doctor, we suppose that there can be some, as you would call it, adjudication placed against the doctor. There will be judgments aplenty, and for many Earth years to come, regarding this issue, and it will grow in its magnitude with the advent of the new viroidal strains and such until the realization and discovery of how to counter them is accomplished in the years ahead.

The point being simply this: When there cannot be those present to give hope, when the life pattern has been disrupted (through choices or lack of choices, through actions or inaction) and the entity, the body, the vehicle of that life pattern or intent becomes a burden greater than its lesson, then perhaps, in terms of the intent of the victim, the more (as you would call it by your own terms, in your own words) the more *humane* method as applied to your domestic animals would certainly seem to be appropriate, if not just as worthy, for those who have no hope.

We are servants and followers of the Master, the Christ … utterly so. And so we must counter our own comment with the following: We know Truth, and we know the Master and His teachings as we know ourselves. Therefore, there is *never* a time without hope. There is never a time wherein a healing is not possible.

In those instances where the entities can bear no more, we shall not judge them, but rather, we shall be among the first here to greet them, to embrace them, to give them hope, to give them comfort, and to give them rest, for they are weary.

You cannot comparatively analyze an entity who has no other path known to them, no other mechanism, who has fallen into such a state of pain and (by their own judgment) inadequacy with someone, conversely, who has all these things and yet willfully terminates their life. No, these are not of the same gradient. These are far apart. See?

We cannot judge the good doctor here, for he perpetuates what he believes in. And whether it shall be considered "right" or "wrong" is a matter that he will search out, perhaps for many Earth years. Thereafter, in these realms, he will carefully examine the soul records of all those he has assisted in that action and where he feels, by his own judgment and analysis, that his work was in any sense in error, then he will make an effort to balance with that in a future life, in a future time, or in another realm. This is not a bad man. This is a good man doing what he believes is best. It is not an action of malicious intent. Nor do we see it at the present as a desire for notoriety, but that he seeks to do or offer what he deems is appropriate. That does not mean that we are judging it aright or wrong. It is all that we see when we look at the entity.

We could sort of rewind the lifetime of these entities and go back over their life, looking for those turns, those decisions, those events that brought them to their point of terminal pain and illness. And perhaps, while so doing, we might also find many other entities whose actions or lack of action did more to terminate that life than this good doctor. See the meaning? He is only dealing with the result of an entire lifetime as it is expressed before him. How many others during that lifetime might have changed that path, or how many others throughout that lifetime might have learned from the example of that terminally ill entity? For not all are without loved ones who have given their all.

And so it could go on here with many more words offered to you in regard to this entity's works, the ramifications of same, and so forth.

Masada

Let us turn for a moment here to what's called Masada, and the entire general topic of what could be called a theological attitude that embraces death over a life of any kind of dominance or lack of freedom to appreciate, to believe, to live, according to their dictums, their tenets. Now, certainly, here there are widely varied factions involved. Some of the groups clearly would be seen to be quite radical (by the analysis of the Earth and, indeed, from here, as well). So we would ask, gently, softly: What is the intent? See how often, how constant, the intent is a key factor in the decision-making process? What is the ideal? The purpose? The goal?

In many of these, as they could be called, *cults* or such, the intent is moreso to dominate and control than it is to empower its followers, to free those who are previously in bondage of some sort (be that theological, mental, emotional, or literal physical bondage). So, if the intent is, as such, to dominate, then clearly this is a misguided, a sort of philosophically entranced group. And, of course, the fault lies with those who seek to dominate and the falseness of their intent as predicated to their followers.

And for the followers, who have only belief as their fault and then take their life, if there are none present to be the mirror of example that there is greater than this limited, dominating belief, then, certainly, the followers are not at fault. And theirs is the opportunity, given not out of a massive need on their part (as with the leaders, this would be the case) but rather, because, perhaps, they were misled. They did fall prey to a misshapen ideal.

Now, Masada is different. It is not, as such, that this leader or that dominated, in that sense, but the theological spirit or belief was and still is the dominating factor. The belief that life and the desecration of all that was held sacred by these entities, fiercely so, would be so vile, so utterly unacceptable under the domination of the conquerors, that to allow that to be perpetuated would, indeed, be a sacrilege, a violation of their oath to God … not to mammon, not to a physical leader in the Earth, but to their individual oath to God.

There were those of the Essenes who were a part of this (though not all), and among these entities there was the offer to extricate a portion, if not the greatest portion, of those who were within the area called Masada. Perhaps if there is any fault at all, it would be this one small aspect: that they chose not to separate but to remain together, to live together or to die together.

We can state with some considerable certainty (and permission here) that all of these entities knew prior to entry (as did many hundreds of thousands of entities like them in those times, and the years which followed) that they knew of this as a possibility (the persecution, and so forth) prior to entry.

We seek not to judge them nor their decision; but, where there is hope, where there is the faith, the belief, there is the empowerment. Where there is the willingness to endure all in God's name, then there is the potential for seeds to be sown. The action of concluding that opportunity *en masse* precluded any opportunity for any such seeds to be sown.

There were others who were placed under oppression, but endured, and others after them, and others after those and so on, all the way up to your time. And isn't the seed of their hope, their faith, their belief, still flowering and producing after its kind, even today as we speak here through this Channel?

The spirit of oneness with God enables endurance. It enables hope. The fear of opposition, or one's enemies, or limitation, can be countered only with faith. So it could be said that these entities, even though many of the good Essenes offered them a chance for perpetuation, opted to depart. Again, that would be our only comment, and not to be construed here as our judgment of them, only an observation of the facts (as you would call it in the Earth).

CLOSING COMMENTS

Well, we must conclude here for the present, but we certainly offer our prayer, now and throughout, that these comments and words have been of equal spiritual purity as those of the inquirers.

Remember, there is always hope. If you have the ideal, the intent, to do all that you know to do, even when it appears there is naught remaining, perhaps there is one more seed that you might sow in God's Name.

And, when you next return, perhaps you will give thanks that someone before you has sown that seed, that the harvest in this lifetime is bountiful … only to find later that it was *you* who had the courage, the faith, the hope, the ideal, to remain to sow that singular seed.

So is it our prayer that these are seeds of hope for each of you. And if there are further questions in this regard, on this or other such topics, we would, in humbleness, in God's Name be joyful to respond.

May the grace and blessings of our Father's wisdom ever be that lamp to guide your footsteps. Fare thee well then for the present, dear friends.

Reading Four:

Life

After Death

This reading was given February 23, 1985.

—

AL MINER/CHANNEL: This reading is a part of the continuing research efforts.

The questions that I'm about to read regarding this topic have been prepared by the people who are interested in this further study and further knowledge, and we wish to thank them for their efforts on behalf of all of us who will hear or read this reading.

QUESTIONS

1. Lama Sing, please describe to us the process of death and the afterlife for an average person on Earth at this time in the Earth's evolvement. What does he or she experience?

2. Would you then compare and contrast this to the process of death and the afterlife experience of a person who has strong Earthly desires and is actively malicious? For example, a person who is addicted to alcohol and drugs and has raped or murdered people?

3. Would you then compare and contrast this to the process of death and the afterlife of the spiritual adept, a person who is spiritually adept.

We further ask that you would please include comments on the following when you are speaking about the above: the process of release from the body; movement through what we call the "tunnel"; the effect of the funeral, prayers, and grief on the person who has died and perhaps the lack of same, should that be the case; guides or teachers; reunion with friends or loved ones; clothing or attire that might be worn by the person who has passed over; review of the past records; choice of future activities; the sash; work back with the Earth or in involvement with the Earth; the relationship of the entity with God and the Light.

Are they more aware of God than they were on Earth? How do they decide on rebirth or reincarnation? How do they prepare for rebirth? How do they advance to other realms and how do they choose those realms? And, also, we ask that you include any other comments that might be helpful or of interest to us that perhaps we may not have asked.

LAMA SING COMMENTARY

Yes, we have the Channel, then, and as well those references which apply to the topic now at hand.

OPENING COMMENTS & ANSWERS

We find the topic and the viewpoint of same to be of some considerable benefit and well chosen, for as one understands the passage from one realm of existence to yet another, perhaps, then, the way (as it is made leading to same and beyond) might be brightened and made more joyful. This, then, would be our humble prayer to each of you.

We shall, as permitted through your grace, change somewhat the order as you have presented it, for we would find that the movement would be a bit more logical and more joyful if we might consistently move upwards, in terms of the vibrational acceptance, which is as to say, in relativity to the consciousness of the entities and the conditions, as you have requested them in your questions.

So we progress, then, beginning with the transition, the movement, of an entity who has been less than joyful, less than loving and kind to others and to themselves, after which we shall move to that which you have called average, and then to that of the entity considered the adept or initiate.

Transition Experience #1

One Who Has Been Less Than Loving and Kind

Come with us, then, on this brief journey, for we now meet one of our brothers, who is watching over (as a guide) an entity about to depart from the Earth.

The location is in the North American, though we might have chosen any such continent or location in the Earth. The city is Chicago, Illinois. It is a bit brisk here, for which Chicago is noted. The entity is huddled there. See? In the dark passageway, in a corner. There are some containers, mostly empty. Some of them contain refuse. There are no others present.

The entity has girded up his clothing. That is, he has bundled up his clothing in an attempt to warm his body against the external elements, the chill. But little can warm that which is within him, for he is at this state, not only in a state of dis-ease (failure of the cleansing and the digestive organs, primarily) but literally the loss of a will or purpose to continue this existence.

This one was in a different state of consciousness at one time in this Earth life, but out of an inability to meet an opportunity, the entity became ever moreso drawn to methods of escape or liberation from that, as he considered it overwhelming and filled with a sense of failure. Thus the entity's pathway should be familiar to many of you who have heard of such or known of such.

Here, the entity, in tattered garb with no one physically present, struggles to continue to live, even though there is no purpose, no will before him.

There are two of the Angelic Host, just off to the side there, summoned forth out of prayer on the part of those who have loved and do love this entity, but know not of his whereabouts. These entities are emissaries of the prayer, the power of prayer, and they are present to prevent there being an infringement upon the entity's own soul consciousness. This occurs when an entity has been prayed for or has prayer around them.

Without same, conditions here and as we shall describe them as the entity moves from the Earth and beyond might be, indeed, different. (We shall be mindful to comment on that as we progress.)

Look at how the entity is saddened by his own consciousness. Look, as you feel what we are describing.

His back is to a small alcove, or corner, of roughly constructed red brick. Several layers of corrugated paper (cardboard, we believe you call this) are over him from the lower portion up to about midway in the chest, but his strength is waning and he can no longer cling to this, thus it has shifted and one foot is exposed. The other, we can see through the paper, is rather twisted and turned upwards, pressing against the wall, as though to push or to force himself somehow or other back into a state of health. The same pressure he applies with his back against the wall.

His right arm and hand are all but useless now, the left still clutches at the lapels of a tattered and worn grayish-colored garment, a jacket. He has a low-profile, long-billed cap over the head, and the sleeve of some garment wrapped around the neck as a muffler or the like. There are only bits of laces in the footwear, tied every so often. The trousers do not match the upper garment, and there are waddings of paper stuffed into the legs of same, as though, we presume, to insulate. The entity is muttering something … the names of those he has known, almost as though some consciousness within him is remembering those things which he has forgotten for the last several-fold Earth years.

As we turn away from the entity and look down the passageway, we see more containers. And darkness. And, at the end, we see light and movement, even though at this moment it is evening. There is a street, and vehicles and entities are moving to and fro, totally unaware of this entity's presence. The sounds can be heard, familiar to this man even at this moment, for he has traversed this pathway, this street, so often, seeking a small pittance here and there to satiate his desire, and has performed all manner of action, including violent actions against others, that he might gain the means by which he could escape, as it were, his own consciousness.

How can it be that the consciousness of those entities just beyond, barely fifty foot-measures away from this entity, cannot feel this soul's cry? How can it be that they hear not nor recognize the song of this soul, as it seeks to enlighten itself?

Turning again, our brother who has brought us here, this one's guide, indicates now that the entity is near to release of the body. The physiological functions are concluded. The life-force reviews the life as it is present, and releases same. Fear is rampant here, emotion is as a burst of energy. The entity stumbles and rolls out of the body, struggling to discover what has occurred.

Other entities quickly appear all around us. The Angelic Host moves swiftly to surround this event, essentially, in a perimeter of light, and we can see beyond such, the many faces and souls who are expressed as limited entities in this realm of consciousness, those entities who are yet bound to the Earth by some carnal desire, by some fear, some doubt, some limitation, by some opportunity yet unaccomplished.

Almost instantly thereafter, other entities (which could be called) *of the Light* appear, and the gathering of Angelic Host begins to dissipate as they seek to find those among the earth-bound entities on the outer perimeter who might now seek to be freed from their own limitation. A song is heard of prayer, and gradually we find that the Angelic Hosts begin to depart, leaving in their stead a feeling of warmth and light, and of comfort and tranquility. The brother, the guide, then, uses this as a material substance, essentially as a balm, to begin to soothe and bring a state of rest to this man who has just left the physical body.

The body is yet there, still grasping the collar, but now in a relaxed state. As we turn to the entity again, whom we shall call Zeke, he holds the collar of his present garment, not unlike that of his coat.

Two others appear and are now behind Zeke, and begin

to perform a certain work, which can by its nature, bring a state of ease. It is not unlike massage in the Earth, though it is performed in a different means. Zeke, becomes increasingly calm, and begins to fall into what you would recognize as a state of sleep. As he so does, the surroundings begin to fade and we are no longer in the presence of the narrow passageway. No longer are the sounds and sensory perceptions of the activities in the street just beyond evident to us but, rather, there is the increasing sound of a gentle breeze, as though passing through a forest or through the tree tops, a sound of gentle water and, faintly, the quiet communications of animals, of birds.

This is a memory of this entity, Zeke's, childhood, the most pleasant of which these guides can find with which to soothe him. We see Zeke now resting upon the bank of a gentle stream somewhere in Indiana as a child of about eight or ten Earth years, not doing anything except allowing the sun's rays to warm him as he contemplates the waters moving past and as he dangles one foot carelessly over the tree root upon which he rests, occasionally touching the water and studying the ripples as they move outward gradually vanishing. As his consciousness focuses in this joyful and restful state upon those ripples that focal point is used to carry him beyond the point of his just-previous departure. So it is a fixational point, so to say, of calm and tranquility not unlike focal points that you use in the Earth plane when meditating or the like.

Zeke is in a totally restful state now. The two entities who were helping him are now seated just beyond, one to the right shoulder and one to the left. Our brother stands on the right side of the entity Zeke and is performing a work, which you would recognize as prayer. He is actually focusing the spiritual strength of this entity, aiding the entity in bringing forth his highest consciousness.

While this is being done, we will explain several things, in answer to your questions, which are truly worthy. The entity's clothing or garb, initially, was that identical to that which his physical body wore, though, you see, they were neither tattered nor worn nor soiled, but pure and created instantly out of the pure energies of God, replicating that which he did wear physically moments before.

This entity, Zeke, had little difficulty in transition for, for many Earth months if not Earth years previous to his departure, he had oft been beyond the realm of consciousness and dwelling in realms beyond the Earth. Not having awareness of his body, curiously not being limited by possession, by material good, nor concerned over any particular matter, the entity was often free of such potentially limiting factors. (You'll understand this better when we find one of average nature to speak thusly about.)

Here, Zeke has found a state of true peace, of true rest, the first he's had for many Earth years, for shortly after the scene we've described to you as the young boy by the water's edge, one of the parents quickly passed from the Earth (that is, was deceased or, made his transition). Zeke's entire life to that point had been joyful, pleasant, though arduous, was in a state of harmonious joy and the future was certain and logically planned.

Shortly thereafter, he and the mother were forced to liquidate the farm and all their worldly goods and move to a city, whereupon the mother sought employment as best she could, forcing her to leave Zeke in the care of others while she found what work she could, for these, you see, were very difficult times, those times of the Depression as you know it in North America.

Here, then, the entity sought out a substitute for the joy, the peace, the beauty of his life, and found little of this in the manner to which he was accustomed. Indeed, he found himself ostracized by his peers because of his uncomely nature and his (as seen) backward way. The entity quickly learned how to manipulate and to control, and how to succeed through devious and mischievous ways.

Thus, a rather abrasive and troubled lifetime ensued. Though the entity rose to some considerable success, materially speaking, possessed wealth, was troubled nonetheless, for the means by which the entity gained these were not comfortable to his spirit, and thus this inner turmoil. Even though outwardly he appeared to be joyful and even though he cast an illusion of some normalcy, some success, the entity grew more and moreso troubled, and gradually turned to various means, artificial, through which to escape same.

Our brother here sought in that time, as the entity's guide, to gain his attention, and to help him find himself and to forgive himself, but those forces which sought to further their own limitation, to satiate their own desires, were also present. Since the guide is bound by Universal Law, he was required to only present this as an alternative choice to Zeke. It seemed quicker and easier to Zeke to turn unto these artificial means: some alcoholic beverages, some activities beyond this, and various ways which allowed him moments of forgetfulness of his own judgment upon himself.

Even so, our brother followed him and stood by him, even until those last moments as you saw him in the narrow passageway. (Thus it was given by the Master, that *Ye shall never be alone,* that *I am always with thee.*) So our brother waited, and sought, through those means which were permitted, to reach Zeke. But the pathway became a deeper descent until he reached an abyss of despair, consuming himself for greater and greater periods of Earth time in a stupor-like state wherein he found friendship, though of a curious sort to most entities' minds.

It should be pointed out here that judgment and guilt, fear and inhibition, tend to bring together entities of like mind and attitude, and there is a camaraderie among these, no different than the camaraderie, the spiritual bond, between entities who seek and who are in the Light. For the soul in each entity will ever strive for fellowship and harmony as a way of life, as a way of expression.

Thus, Zeke's success, his family and children and associates, were released, perhaps not by his conscious choice, but by his unconscious activities. And yet they looked for him. And yet they found, after his body was no longer his living temple, their beloved Zeke.

So while we are watching here, let us observe the activities in the Earth plane of consciousness:

His body, decimated by the years of his activities, has been determined to be best prepared through cremation, and that is well, for the memory of the entity will live on in the heart, not in the visual, and the bonds will be easier released in such a manner. (This is oft best in such instances, see?)

The greatest grief is for the eldest daughter, who is born of his own soul group. The mate's sadness is actually lightened by the location and consummation of this bond. It is not to say that she has no love for him, for that is not correct, but that the fear, the doubt, the hope, can now be placed in proper accord and her life's joy can be totally freed once again. She gives her prayer and her blessing and does it well, for it is received here as a rush of light and sound, beautiful to behold as it now swirls around this gathering and intensely around the entity, Zeke. He is visibly stirred by the prayer and it seems to bring out a hidden beauty in his appearance. His garb begins to change and the darkness of the fabric lightens greatly, its pattern begins to change.

His mother renews an old grief, the former loss of Zeke's father, and her prayer is a sobbing one. (It is heard here moreso as a chant, a mantra, a tonal quality moreso likened unto a heavy, in your terms, classical passage rather than a light aria, as the mate's prayer was moments ago.) With its presence, a flickering of pain is seen on Zeke's facial expression and a moment of darker hue appears in the clothing, but quickly blends with the lighter presence of his mate's prayer and the light of his guide nearby and is blended to make his garments a bit more radiant. For in the last moments of his mother's prayer, she remembers the small child she so often found by the bank of the small stream, blissfully seeing the future potential in the surface of the passing water. It warmed her heart and it freed her prayer, and she departed from the ceremony with that as her final thought, and that prayer, then, instantaneously became as the breath of life born in the spring in the Earth.

There is, yet, the elder daughter. We shall call her Maria. The sadness from this entity is indescribable. (We find ourselves burdened by its presence.) Our brother beckons to us to assist him. Two move to the right and left shoulder of Zeke, radiating light to him, as we take a position opposite our brother, placing Zeke between us, with another at his feet. With the combined strength of our group, we intensify the light, striving simultaneously to reflect it back to Maria to not only prevent there from being limitation to Zeke, but to contribute to a sister who is one of Maria's guides.

Maria is served, being calmed, by the presence of our sister, her guide, and through the efforts of this group, as well. We are protectively preventing, as we are permitted, any injurious subliminal effect or residual effect upon Zeke by the grief or the transmission of energy from Maria. Over the next several Earth days and in the future, Maria shall be guided to stimulate intent or purpose … direction, so to say, of her life energies. Others who are a part of Maria's soul group will assist our sister by contributing unto Maria's pathway by working within what is called the flexible or malleable, the alternative, influences in the Earth, which we have a right to work within as long as we do not interfere with the Free Will. (These are intermediary passages, which do not violate the *spherical*, as it might be called, domain of the individual entity. It is in the area which would be called *neutral energy* often relative to mass-thought, often relative to the native forces, the Spirit of God. Only those souls who have gained certain consciousness are enabled and rightful to work therein, sufficiently demonstrative of their ability to control their own thoughts and/or emotions so as to not disrupt the order and the rightful progression of that dimension. See? But you'll likely ask questions on that some other Earth time, with a note of loving humor.)

We'll accelerate this a bit now, for Zeke has fallen into a state of rest and may remain there for several Earth years, by your measure. What will occur is, Zeke will move from this state of rest, during which, we might add, he will pass through all the experiences that he has had in the past, so as he is prepared to so do. His brother, his guide, will be with him, expressing himself in whatso'er consciousness Zeke chooses.

At the moment when Zeke asks for assistance, his guide will be there to bring him back to his spiritual form, whereupon he will be awakened. Until that time (indeterminable, but by the will of Zeke) he will remain in a state of limited consciousness, made so by his own limited ability to forgive himself, and by the judgments, the guilts, or burdens which he imposes upon himself, *and* (take note of this) which are imposed upon him by others in the Earth, whether they be thoughts of grief at his loss behind which there is the intent of love, or whether they be thoughts of anger, of judgment, of hatred, or whatnot. He must meet all of this. To do so, he will seek a level of expression which will be equivalent to his own ability, his own level of acceptance. Fortunately, he has been protected to an extent through the action of prayer; and that prayer will remain around him (you will recall, as the light, the sphere around him) and it will keep him.

Otherwise, his last remembered thoughts might have drawn him so strongly into the Earth consciousness that when he tumbled out of his body and looked around bewilderingly, he might have risen, walked down the passageway and out onto the street, attempting once again to solicit funds or to do acts which would gain him the opportunity to gain drink, to gain alcohol. He would have quickly found that no one paid attention to him.

After a passage of some time of frustration and agony, he would have discovered that he could satiate his own desires by entering those dwelling places where other entities yet in physical body were doing as he would do were he yet in physical form. He may have passed into and out of their presence, physically, and experienced as they experienced. And as long as they were satiating their cravings willingly, his presence would have contributed to and furthered their urge, their own limitation. Thus, those who have eyes to see, ears to hear, senses to sense, will find in and about such places the presence of such entities as we have just defined as the potential for Zeke. But, as we have given, prayer has preserved him.

At the moment Zeke freed himself from the limited form, that prayer became effective. You will note it did not interfere with him, but it did protect him from those who were satiating themselves through him while he was in physical body. If they could have reached Zeke, he would have become one of them, and dwelled within what we would call *the Sea of Faces*: entities or souls bound to the Earth because of their own limitation, and destined to remain there until one such illuminated moment of agony, wherein they would cry out to be freed. Instantly a guide, a sister, a teacher, a brother, would whisk them from that level of consciousness, essentially in a sphere of light to protect and preserve, and would have borne him, like as not, unto a realm similar to this where we now are present with him.

His clothing has changed to that of a garb moreso of what we would call moderate or mundane. It is the best he can surmise and it is the best esteem he has of himself. It's a coarse fabric, not at all pleasant to wear, irritating to the dermal, the skin. The colors are dull and lackluster. That is not the true nature of his garb, but that's what he believes and that's what he accepts and so that is what he's wearing. It has no sash, no cord, which would be indicative of a certain level of spiritual accomplishment, a certain awareness, and not having such befits the realm in which he shall dwell for an undetermined period of Earth time, until he is ready to move on.

What shall ultimately occur, we are told by our brother, is that Zeke will come forth from this, to be sure. It will be to answer a cry of agony from another entity not unlike himself in the just-previous incarnation, who will so move him, will be so strong, as to draw him from his own limitation to claim his spiritual truth in order to answer that call and to protect that entity. The entity's name is, and shall be in that time in future, Maria.

It is beautiful, is it not, dear friends?

Together, then, they shall find their way; and they shall know themselves to be of the same soul vibration and to be that which you would call souls of the same fabric, the polarization of one consciousness. For Maria shall search, Earth year after Earth year, to find that which brought her the joy she knew in her father's presence, a certain warmth and gladness of heart merely by the presence of his consciousness and by a momentary touch of his hand to her forehead. Not finding same, she too shall change her ways, and turn to what she deems to be a method of escape from continual frustration and unsatisfied desires.

Transition Experience #2:

One Who Lived an Average Life

Here is an entity now coming forth whose light is balanced. The entity has just departed the Earth after a full and rich lifetime compared to Zeke's. Not having been successful to any great measure, only those who personally knew the entity are likely to remember this soul, this entity. Even they will remember for only a time, and then the memory shall fade, only to be recalled on certain occasions or under certain stimuli.

We could call the entity *average*, in the sense that we see that his intent was to do well, always intending to do much more than he ever accomplished. There were those times here and there where he moderated his intent, his purpose, and those conditions and activities were such to have had an impact upon him. This entity we shall call Phillip.

We find in him a love for working with the hands, a sense of fondness with wood, with constructing things. Phillip, also dwelling in the mid-western portion of the North American, lived in the same approximate locale for the entirety of his lifetime, took to mate and bore family, and saw to their needs and comforted them. His support and attendance in religious matters could be considered proper. His affairs in terms of his community and his associations with others were of some warmth and some supportiveness. He was given to spontaneous celebration on occasion, for which his mate would often chastise him, and for which he would often seek to make amends. (This we find with a note of loving humor.)

He had a companion, a small canine (dog, in your colloquial terms) of which he was very fond. The dog's name was Specter, and the dog is present here as a life-form, awaiting his loved one's proximity and consciousness of his presence.

Also accompanying Phillip are two souls. These are family members he knew in past: one, very closely, a grandfather; the other one, a twice-removed aunt, as it were. Phillip is first puzzled by their presence, not having recognized his own departure, for his departure was during a period of sleep, thus the struggle with the physical body was not profound. (It is commented to here that perhaps we should have found one who was conscious and had struggle with relieving themselves of the physical body. Well, no matter. If there is interest in that, ask it and we'll seek one out, see?) But here, Phillip initially became a bit confused at the appearance of these entities, who at first he had forgotten were deceased. "Deader than a stone," he says, and his speech to them is (in the most paraphrased of colloquial terms) one of utter amazement, and these entities strive humorously and with good cheer to moderate and to soften the obvious effect.

Turning to view his own physical form yet in a state of sleep (for the body is not completely released as yet), there is a visible trail of light, which more or less undulates from Phillip in the conscious state here to Phillip in the physical state. You see, he hasn't noticed that yet. He rushes over to his physical body and grasps it by the shoulders, attempting to shake it, finding only that his hands pass immediately through the body and he grasps nothing. Jumping back in abject horror, he turns to his former relatives and throws himself into his grandfather's arms, whereupon he is immediately given an energy, a light, and the emotion transcends from one of intensity to a feeling of warmth and calm.

He pushes himself back from his grandfather's embrace, a bit embarrassed, to look into the eyes of someone totally different. Not finding himself holding his grandfather anymore, but rather a very beautiful female entity, he is a bit befuddled here.

At that point, Specter appears, and we find the expression of joy to be one of sheer delight on the part of both. It is a small, basically white, black-spotted dog, a bit gaunt, but then, it ran a lot with Phillip as it was its delight to do on evening walks. So it leaps into Phillip's arms and the reunion is a sight of joy and true blessing.

Turning again to the entity he had just embraced, he asks, "Who are you?" whereupon she, with a smile and radiance of the eyes sufficient to melt a heart constructed of ice, speaks in a sound which is unlike any that Phillip has heard in past to his recall, for it vibrates within him with a resonance of utter joy and warmth. She states simply, "I, Phillip, am an old friend, someone who has been, and is, very fond of you."

It seems to have such an impact upon Phillip that he can neither think of any further question nor has he need of any further answer.

All the while, off to the side, there is that great-aunt, just standing as though she were not at all appropriate in this presence, yet we can see in the eyes that she is far more than the appearance would imply, for there is in the eyes the wisdom and the spiritual light of one from a higher realm.

So, as Phillip and Specter and the new-found friend from the past slowly turn and begin to walk in what appears to be an upward direction, more or less unknowingly on the part of Phillip, for he is consumed by the radiance of the one next to him, whose hand he grasps. And they begin a dialogue of conversation of no profound meaning, but merely, as we see them, of reorienting their energies and reawakening a consciousness between them. The great-aunt more or less dutifully following behind, as they move upwards in this tunnel-like passageway of light.

As we peer, moving behind them at a respectable distance, outside of this tunnel of light, we see many darker hues of the various realms of consciousness and limitation through which we are passing in this journey. The journey could have been made instantaneously, in your terms, but it will be more acceptable to Phillip in this way, for he believes he must walk to get to one place from another.

We will abort time a bit here and find them in the future. A moment please ...

Very well, we are some two to three Earth years advanced from the previous. Phillip is now wearing a garment which is of some silver or whitish color. It is not completely a solid color; it has various other swatches of colors, as if hovering over an undergarment of pure white. The sash is there with two cords in it, but it has many loose fibers, as though they are not completely woven as yet and as though the knots in the sash are to keep them from unraveling or to show where the weaving has left off. It is worn about midway, but moreso towards the right, frontally, as though to be a reminder.

His companion is still present here and is in her full spiritual garb, which is of a brilliant white color. The sash is golden and is worn completely to the right, signifying the accomplishment. (We are not permitted to see whether it is entwined and braided or not, for we have not the right to so perceive. Though we know the entity well here, we must be of clarity and advise that we are not permitted to reveal.)

Phillip's great-aunt, as it were, has also changed the garb, and now stands as a tall entity, whose countenance is now of the masculine energy, fair in appearance. The robe is woven of a somewhat different fabric, luminescent, as though it possesses a light, which by its nature or quality seems to generate its own color, actually a blending of colors, though its hue seems to be a fiery reddish, bluish white.

(There is some humor here, for the combination of colors described do not physically combine into recognizable hues in the Earth plane. In other words, blended in the Earth, they wouldn't appear as such. Well, we aren't in the Earth, see? There is a moment of considerable mirth here, largely with us as the focal point. That is well, and we are joyful.)

Then we should describe the garment as a basically white, or pure, garment through which there are minute pinnacles of alternating red and blue colors or emanating light. (Ah, yes, that's much better.) The cord on his garment, or the sash, is of the purest silver-white color, and radiates. This entity is a teacher. He stands yet to the back and a bit above these entities, observing, for Phillip is not yet ready to consider his unlimited nature.

Phillip has Specter yet with him, and they have lots of walks in the meadow and in the glen, and they've met quite a few entities of good cheer. There is a kindly nature here and many are about the same chores or hobbies or tasks as have pleased them while in the Earth plane. Phillip is not fully aware that he can interact with the Earth and so he's not been offered any opportunity to so do, though the female entity, will soon show him certain opportunities … not telling him, of course, what they are, but allowing him to discover them and to learn from the discovery, and thereby to liberate more of his own consciousness.

Phillip will wait, we're told, two to three hundred years before looking at his own records. Thereafter, he may study these and compare them to opportunities used and the opportunities unused in the just-previous lifetime. Then, with others of Light and spiritual strength, will enter and study the Earth and others therein.

After this, he will meet with certain of the brothers, likely one of whom will be the teacher standing off to the side here, and discuss alternatives. Then will meet with the soul group, and then will examine opportunities for re-entry into the Earth (to be reborn or to reincarnate) or to make a decision as to whether or not further involvement at that level of consciousness is the best course of action. Whereupon, he might choose to move to other realms, or to continue from this position serving those whom he is permitted to serve and assisting where he can, studying and existing, being joyful, traveling and experiencing. You see? Not unlike, comparatively speaking, the Earth, but in a much more unlimited sense.

He'll have to deal with a few limitations, which he experienced in the just-previous lifetime, for they are represented as the swatches of colors over his garment that we spoke of earlier. He'll discover their presence and ask about them, and in the asking he'll realize what they are. He'll then return to those experiences, relive them, re-experience them, move away from them for greater perspective, in the companionship of the entities with him, and then, ultimately, analyze this, and try to work through some of it.

Ultimately, he'll work in prayer, we believe. It looks like that will be his choice when he discovers its power. He's done enough of it in the Earth, although with little or no belief in it. But when he sees the work he's done with prayer, we believe he'll turn to that as his next activity.

Likely won't incarnate, then, in the Earth until about 2800, or 2500 at the earliest. Looks like he will make some considerable progress, and may choose to work with others in the meeting and greeting of souls who depart through what you call accident: sudden, momentary decisions offered to them.

Zeke, you will recall, needs a longer period of balance. He will dwell in a realm not unlike Phillip, but it will be limited by his own ability to accept that he could be in a more joyful state. Because of his actions against the Free Will of others in the Earth, whereupon he took from them to meet his own carnal desires, he will now meet that in this realm (though he has the right to refuse it); whereupon it will lie in some abeyance as karma for a future experience; whereupon, from a wiser position of his spiritual consciousness, he will wish to unburden himself of that as a limitation. His work with Maria, in the future, will no doubt relieve him of some karma because he will on several occasions move into a great sense of emotional oneness with her in order to try and help her. In that moment, he will allow himself grace. There, we will join with him and our brothers to attempt to accelerate (if he is willing) that growth, in which case he would not need to meet that karma, and he would be unburdened, allowing him to move to a realm in some proximity to where Phillip is at this moment.

There is no nature within man which is as an automatic mechanism which limits him. The nature of man which limits, is his own cognizance of himself. (That's, of course, true for *woman* as well. We are speaking in terms of man as mankind, or souls in the Earth. We don't have a great deal of concern in the finality whether that's male or female, with a note of loving humor.) So the effort in these realms, then, is to extricate the consciousness from its own limitation by way of showing, by way of demonstrative activities. Then through the activities which can stimulate a certain spark, a certain ray of hope or light even within the darkest of entities' consciousness, which will draw forth a momentary desire to help, an instant of compassion, an instant of selflessness. Then, all of the kingdom of God will be offered to them in that moment, and to the extent that they can perceive and accept, that they shall be given.

You ponder this: How can it be that an entity in the greatest depths of despair, in a moment of selflessness could be offered all the greatest in the creation of God's consciousness when there are others who laboriously struggle through lifetime after lifetime, meeting and working through each aspect karmicly, trudging steadfastly forth upon a pathway, seemingly unending, yet ever upward in its movement? How can this be right, you might ask. What teacher, dear friends, has written that you must dwell for an indeterminate length of time in a certain consciousness or experience in order to gain from it? Is it not righteous that one extreme be countered with another? Is it not written that the last shall be first? Go forth, then, and seek within self the deepest moment of despair within your consciousness, and know that in that moment, that the entirety of our Father's kingdom is offered to you; and that through your own graceful willingness to accept, you are instantly extricated from that depth and raised to that place on high. It is your soul's potential. It is the potential of every soul.

Phillip has chosen his pathway, much of that choice yet not known to him. Zeke has chosen his. Again, much of that unknown to him. How does all of this compare, for example, to an entity who might know of their pathway, who *consciously* has traveled it?

We'll explore that as our next joyful venture.

Transition Experience Three:

One Who Walked in Life as an Adept

Man's consciousness … How wondrous is its potential! Through the mind of man one can perceive any existence he would have. There can be the action and reaction, predicated by stimuli or emotion, as infinite as man's own ability to envision. There is the potential of creativity and inventiveness, ingeniousness, limited only by the spheres of the dreamer, the visionary; the body of man, recognized by some to be a temple wherein a Force Eternal dwells and from which it may spring forth on missions of its own choice (essentially at will), wherein one in a rightful conscious state might move from the body, perceive and do. So, then, does an entity in such a possession of consciousness become known as one called *an adept.*

An adept is an entity who has knowledge of, and has begun the practice thereof (in order to gain a perspective of), his true and complete nature.

An adept may be recognized by some or by none, dependent upon the will of that entity. An adept can walk in the pathway of the average entity, called Phillip or in the pathway of an entity called Zeke. The actions and attitudes would be different, but it would be the work that would be important to the adept that would have caused them to choose that way of life. They would not be bound, as Zeke, but they would be present, using a spiritual strength to overcome any present limitation, and using their physical presence to be encouraging and supportive where opportunity presented itself.

In the role or walk of life as with the entity Phillip, here we would find the entity might become inventive, creative, might speak out against that which he sees as limiting, and might be a bit more active in the performance and belief of prayer. And, if truly aware of his own adeptness (or hers), might gradually move into a way of life which is more demonstrative of that consciousness which the entity holds.

And then there is another expression that the adept might choose, and that is wherein the entity expressed in physical form chooses to become a channel of blessings. That entity, in the stages of adeptness, yet might struggle with this or that as an illusion or limitation, but more oft than not, not out of necessity, but out of choice: that there might be the better understanding at the physical level, the emotional level, and somewhat the mental level, of the opportunities or challenges that face their brethren.

The adept has no true purpose in remaining in Earth, except that the knowledge of the adept is such that to remain therein is to remain in service. The adept, likely, has aspects of knowledge which they know can be amplified best of all by expressing themselves in the Earth, and has soul work or soul purpose unto which they are committed, which are also furthered therein.

The adept is never alone in the sense of companionship, and more oft than not has knowledge of that presence and of that company. The adept may see and may know beyond the perception of the five senses and may bring forth that knowledge in an expressive way, which is loving and kind and which is of a service to all who would seek.

The adept becomes a master when there is the transition of all those limitations, and the knowledge which was sought after becomes expressed and thus is as wisdom, and liberates the entity from the final illusions. Not to say that the adept has that potential each moment, though it is present. The adept generally chooses a certain form of limitation in order that the consciousness remains sufficiently in the Earth, that the expression of those energies and that consciousness needed most in Earth, would be provided a pathway.

Now then, since we have defined what we would consider an adept, a practitioner, let us consider your questions.

Here's an entity whose consciousness is familiar with movement from the physical to realms beyond, and knows that that which is called the *tunnel of light* or the passageway of light is more or less a connective filament or firmament, a silver cord or whatnot, which connects their highest potential and their source of infinite flow in all respects to their more finite expression in the physical. In that knowledge they are aware that they can command this and are intended to so do, as they are requested to so do.

We have not an adept who is transiting from the Earth at this moment. Thus, we have asked a brother to re-experience their movement for you. We give great thanks unto this brother, for her loving kindness, her charity, and her spiritual light. We have switched the connotation from brother to the feminine, for the entity was in a female body in those times just past, now known to us here as a part of the brethren, or as a brother. (We cheerfully commented moments ago about a sister. That, of course, we believe was obvious to you as an attempt at good cheer and mirth, for such is not needed here, though it is a rightful choice if it is made. See?)

So, this entity not only taught, but was one of whose hands were the instrument of her work. Dedicated in faith and in commitment to God and to the man known as Jesus, the entity served whereso'er she was asked. The earliest portion of her life was, by the measure comparatively of Earth, a struggle. Existence in the Earth plane, by the standard or expectation of others was, at best, painful, for the entity found as often as she would attempt to live in a manner expected of her, to perform and be of such a nature as was anticipated, this then was always a great effort, leading ultimately to a condition of unrest, of displeasure, a lack of harmony.

Then as we see her moving through that lifetime, we find that this continual, we might call it, frustration, or sense of incompleteness, caused her (not to turn to, as Zeke, alcohol) but to turn within herself, to find the source of what it is or was that she was seeking. Therein she found a light, a beauty, which came forth and spoke to her. At first, startling. She questioned it, challenged it, turning with reverence to the orthodox ordered church, and to that called the Holy Book. The voice continued, assuring and supporting, encouraging her to search among those two sources.

Finally the entity, in a time of great need, rushed to the side of a friend injured in an automobile accident and began to pray at the unconscious side of the friend, caressing and soothing her around the head and facial area, where there had been extensive cranial damage through concussion and spinal shock, some movement of fluids and rupture in the brain, condition worsening by the moment (category three or four, we believe). Anyway, the entity's reverent and fond love for this friend caused her once again to reach deep within herself. While praying and caressing her friend, the voice spoke, "If you believe unto Me, then do My work," whereupon she literally froze in her actions. Her body trembled with a confusing sensory feeling of heat and cold, as though an electrical current were welling up within her and began to radiate itself down her hand yet, unknowingly, placed upon the forehead of her friend.

She could see and feel this column of light as it moved slowly down the upper arm, the elbow, the forearm, and then the hand itself began to glow, first white, now yellow, now green, beautiful in its hue. First, remaining superficially around her hand and over the facial area of her friend, now gradually her friend taking on that hue, and her aura blending with that color, slowly at first. Finally, we see this encompassing her friend and the color beginning to race, cycling around in great swirling motions, now more colors, more variations.

All the while, this our friend, our adept, transfixed by

the entire matter … thought-less, emotion-less, spellbound by the experience. An indeterminate amount of time passes and finally our adept begins to feel the energy as though it seems to be drawing back into her, the brilliance subsiding, settling to a soft, golden-white glow around her friend. And she hears the words, "It is done."

Gathering herself up from the experience, on the third Earth day, her friend awoke from the comatose condition and called for her, "Ruth! Ruth!" Whereupon, the adept moved to her side, dropping to her knees in a joyful, sobbing prayer. Her friend spoke only these words, "Thank you, Ruth, thank you," and then she fell into a peaceful sleep. Her body, thereafter recovering, she became whole again, to the marvel and wonderment of those attending her.

Most all who heard of or were a part of this event claimed it to be some sort of spontaneous reparatory remission, using elongated terms to suffice to cover their disbelief at her recovery. No matter. Those who had eyes to see looked at the entity Ruth with awe and with fondness. Others merely went about their own affairs. But unto the adept, a moment of truth, a moment of purification. From that moment forward this entity, whom we have called Ruth, no longer walked in a state of darkness. From this point forward, she became ever moreso illuminated, and ever moreso brought into service in the Father's name. She was awakened at some thirty-seven-odd years of existence in the Earth to become a servant of that joyous light from which she had sprung forth. Thereafter, all whom she met were blessed by her love and by the supportive encouragement found so often flowing abundantly unto any who would ask.

So then, as that life came unto its conclusion (with many other experiences certainly worthy of note, but too lengthy to retell here), the entity's consciousness now moves into that state which is beyond the physical senses, and the body begins to radiate a glow, a warmth. This warmth is as an energy summoning itself up upon itself, and when it begins, the entire body can be detected as having this energy. Slowly, it seems to move up the body coming together upon itself until we are at the solar plexi region, and then the energy turns inward upon itself and intensifies, ever more brilliant. The entity's consciousness then moves from the physical body, and the body is shortly thereafter released from its service.

There is no pain, save that which is or was normal in the sense of her willingness to accept the same burdens as her brethren, but only to the extent she chose to so do from a certain level of consciousness. Why, you might ask. In order to serve, even in that state, certain souls who could not accept death, for there are those souls in all levels of consciousness limited by their own illusion, by their own fear. The adept is always in service, whereso'er they dwell and whatso'er circumstance may prevail upon them. Theirs is a way of joyful truth and wondrous discovery, for in their consciousness there is the knowledge that joy is a constant companion, not momentary, not designated for this portion of life and not that, but constant. Thus, they claim their heritage and choose to be in joyous service continually, whether awake or in slumber, in life or in death (as you call it). They are beings of light, learning to know themselves, and discovering in that knowledge or learning process more about their own unlimited nature.

At this point of departure, this entity has not, as yet, gained the level of acceptance, that *self*-acceptance, to become known as what you would call a master; but from the light and the beauty as we see this entity called Ruth, we should think it only moments away. We shall add our blessings and our joyous companionship, so as she shall will it whenso'er as she shall, and we shall be humbled and joyful should we be called.

The entity's departure from the Earth is a moment filled with light. There is a bursting forth in radiant color and sound, which is indescribable in Earthly terms.

The entity's presence in these realms is a cause for celebration, for the entity knoweth unto whence she goes. And those with whom she shall rejoin, she remembers serving well. The Light of our Father is ever-present in its purest brilliance, and creates sound by intermingling with the other sounds and lights emanating from the other entities or souls gathered. There is a wondrous group.

We are in the point of entry, which is transitory to the upper realms. It is a place of brilliant beauty and wondrous joy, the very atmosphere charged with a feeling of love, a feeling of oneness. In the eyes of each of the entities present there can be seen the unmitigated, unrestricted, unlimited, totally-giving attitude of love, as though one would find and welcome self so freely given that tears of joy are swept upon the cheeks of each entity who would see this (were they in form physical).

We cannot view this without singing ourselves, and without allowing our souls to join in with this harmony, and so we pause a moment here. We thank you for your patience and for these moments of blessing here. We shall return …

CLOSING COMMENTS

Thus, we thank thee, dear friends, for your willingness to search out beyond yourselves, and we pray that that as we have given it here during this joyous meeting brings to you a sense of familiarity and understanding which will contribute to your own joyful potential in this, the current life expression in the Earth, and beyond into eternity.

The entity we've called Ruth, now enjoined with us once again here is (as you may have surmised or deduced) a member of what we call "our group" here, one loved completely by all present, and very close in harmony to this Channel. Thus, we would find an even greater joy in the expression of the experiences as we have defined them and a pledge from here to continue with those works as the entity Ruth has performed them in the Earth so as she's permitted in our Father's name from this group to those who would seek in Earth.

But what of the other questions? Did this entity have and does she have guides? Indeed, it is so, for those who guide this entity are those who, through their presence, contribute to her furtherance of growth and joyfulness. Simply because an entity is in a certain state of consciousness in the Earth, this does not mean, nor should it imply, that they are near to the end of some sort of expression or existence; that there is a finiteness to the potentiality for growth; that once one ascends to what is perceived and what is demonstratively expressed as a master in the Earth, that their journey and their joyfulness have concluded; and that they might, from that state, go into some sort of dormancy, having placed aside awaking and their assumption of growth. It is not so!

As one reaches that certain level of understanding, that in and of itself, not only furthers the potential growth and joy, but expands it in an almost arithmetic progression of expansion. For as one has one perception, then two, then three; an *adept* has two, then four, then sixteen! See?

The master moves in multiples. Their contentment and tranquility in the Earth plane while yet in physical body is evidential demonstration of this to you, their ability to transcend and be in harmony and completeness with the smallest particle of existence, and to do the same with the greatest with seemingly an indifferent attitude, consistently joyful and reverent in both instances … the greatest and the least.

The entity's garb is brilliant, at the moment radiating a rosy color, which is transcendent over a beautiful white, pure color beneath. The rose is the emanation of love, the healing grace, the energy which is to reach the very creative fiber of each entity and, indeed, each cell or fiber of each physical body. It is the light of Christ's love; it is the emanation of God-love. This is the predominant color that the entity projects, for this is the predominant area of chosen work that the entity manifests, and this is the purpose of the entity's presence here. Earlier, the cloak, the garment, was a golden yellow, for her intent was to create wisdom by the re-telling of her experience.

The sash is beautiful in its radiance and lustrous in terms of its accomplishments. Again, we shall withhold any in-depth comment for reasons which are not quite completely capable of explanation to you for various reasons at present. We know that there are other questions, and we know that some of the questions or areas of comment you have requested have not been clearly explored here. But we have well used the life-force of this Channel for these works for the present. Thus we shall at this time, in honor and reverence to our brethren who guide us and who watch over the Channel, in a moment, conclude and release him to consciousness in the Earth. But before we do, we offer you these last humble observations:

When you are seeking, know that the potential of each of those who were discussed here during this meeting lies within all of you and all of us, the differentiating or deciding factor being that of one's own willingness to seek beyond themselves. Not to seek in the manner beyond themselves, as Zeke, but in the manner which is the most joyful and most in accord with your spiritual perspective of righteousness.

When you give up, when you relinquish, your right to quest, you are limiting yourself and you are limiting the potential which lies beyond your present lifetime, not eternally but for a time. And you may be casting a certain requirement or mold for the future, which you would choose to fulfill by reincarnating and experiencing these obstacles or challenges once again.

Karma is opportunity. It is not a burden. It is not a debt. It is not a pending blessing. Karma is our Father's grace manifested as opportunity. If you view your karma and forgive, if you are spiritually attuned and see karma properly, in a moment of understanding you can accomplish what is required by others to be fulfilled in the course of an entire lifetime.

So, our message we leave for your thought is to believe unto yourself to be of the Eternal Source. And in the belief, know that it is His intent for you to be joyful, and that as you seek that joy, honorably giving the same rights to others, you contribute by example and raise the consciousness, and thus the potential, for all.

This area of topic is vast. This area of *opportunity* is within you

About Lama Sing

More than thirty years ago, for our convenience, the one through whom this information flows accepted the name Lama Sing, though it was stated they, themselves, have no need for names or titles.

"We identify ourselves only as servants of God, dedicated to you, our brothers and sisters in the Earth." –Lama Sing

About This Channel

"Channel is that term given generally to those who enable themselves to be, as much as possible, open and passable in terms of information that can pass through them from the Universal Consciousness or other such which are not associated in the direct sense with their finite consciousness of the current incarnation." –Lama Sing

BOOKS BY AL MINER & LAMA SING

The Chosen: Backstory to the Essene Legacy
The Promise: Book I of The Essene Legacy
The Awakening: Book II of The Essene Legacy
The Path: Book III of The Essene Legacy

In Realms Beyond: Book I of The Peter Chronicles
In Realms Beyond: Study Guide
Awakening Hope: Book II of The Peter Chronicles
Return to Earth: Book III of The Peter Chronicle

Death, Dying, and Beyond: How to Prepare for The Journey Vol I
The Sea of Faces: How to Prepare for The Journey Vol II

Jesus: Book I
Jesus: Book II

The Course in Mastery

When Comes the Call

Seed Thoughts
Seed Thoughts to Consciousness

Stepstones: Compilation 1

The Children's Story

About Al Miner

A chance hypnosis session in 1973 began Al's tenure as the channel for Lama Sing. Since then, nearly 10,000 readings have been given in a trance state answering technical and personal questions on such topics as science, health and disease, history, geophysical, spiritual, philosophical, metaphysical, past and future times, and much more. The validity of the information has been substantiated and documented by research institutions and individuals, and those receiving personal readings continue to refer others to Al's work based on the accuracy and integrity of the information in their readings. In 1984, St. Johns University awarded Al an honorary doctoral degree in parapsychology.

Al conducts a variety of field research projects, as well as occasional workshops and lectures. He is no longer accepting requests for personal readings, but, rather, is devoting his remaining time to works intended to be good for all. Much of his current research is dedicated to the concept that the best of all guidance is that which comes from within. Al lives with his wife in Florida.

www.ingramcontent.com/pod-product-compliance
Lightning Source LLC
LaVergne TN
LVHW010625100826
845148LV00014B/3120

* 9 7 8 0 9 7 9 1 2 6 2 0 8 *